Diane,

Happy 70th!

Love,

Day

Unpacking My Library: Artists and Their Books

Edited by Jo Steffens and Matthias Neumann

Yale University Press
New Haven and London

Marcel Proust, from "On Reading," translation © 2011 by Damion Searls, reprinted from Marcel Proust and John Ruskin, *On Reading* (Hesperus, 2011).

yalebooks.com/art

Special thanks are offered to the following people: all of the artists, Janet Cardiff, Billy Childish, Mark Dion, Tracey Emin, Theaster Gates, George Bures Miller, Wangechi Mutu, Martin Parr, Ed Ruscha, Carrie Mae Weems; their assistants and gallerists, Zev Tiefenbach, Steve Lowe, Shawna Gallancy, Eimear O'Raw, Alexandra Small, Helena Thompson, Astrid Meek, Mary Dean, Paul Ruscha, Anthony Rossi. Also, Tamara Schechter, Matthew Higgs, Beth Daugherty, Malcolm Mooney, Wayne Baerwaldt, and Paul Yamazaki.

Yve Ludwig, based on a design by Pentagram Design
Set in Neue Haas Unica Pro and Mercury Text
Printed in China by Regent Publishing Services Limited

Photo Credits
Janet Cardiff and George Bures Miller: Yuri Akuney
Billy Childish: Gerald Jenkins
Mark Dion: Elisabeth Smolarz
Tracey Emin: Gerald Jenkins
Theaster Gates: Tom Wagner
Wangechi Mutu: Adi Shniderman
Martin Parr: Gerald Jenkins
Ed Ruscha: Paul Ruscha
Carrie Mae Weems: David Paul Broda (black background) and Anthony Rossi (yellow background)

Library of Congress Control Number: 2017932140
ISBN 978-0-300-21698-1
A catalogue record for this book is available from the British Library.

This paper meets the requirements of ANSI/NISO Z39.48-1992 (Permanence of Paper).

10 9 8 7 6 5 4 3 2 1

Foreword

Books share their fates with their readers.
—Umberto Eco, *The Name of the Rose*

Artists and Their Books is the latest volume in the *Unpacking My Library* series; it follows *Writers and Their Books* (2011) and the progenitor of the series, *Architects and Their Books* (2009). The first volume began life as an exhibit that I devised and produced while director of Urban Center Books, the Municipal Art Society of New York's bookstore for art, architecture, and design. The bookstore, considered one of the best niche stores in the city, featured many hard-to-find, classic, and limited-edition titles.

After many years of providing good books to discerning book lovers, I became intensely curious about the libraries of our patrons. I decided to flip the script and ask them which books they found personally meaningful, with the underlying assumption that a private collection could reveal something about the nature of its owner. For the exhibition I settled on the idea of photographing entire libraries and "stitching" the bookshelves together, in postproduction, to create a scrollable, digital "bookscape" of each architect's collection; a list of the ten books that had most influenced them was also included. Subsequent projects similar to *Unpacking My Library* include Aaron Hicklin's curated bookstore One Grand and the *New York Times*'s weekly "By the Book" column. (The BBC's seminal *Desert Island Discs* radio show, created in 1942, asks guests to choose the eight records they would take to a desert island.)

Yale University Press saved *Unpacking My Library* from its digital fate, and the resulting printed monographs are the ultimate tribute to the enduring value of the book as a container for human imagination. Walter Benjamin's essay "Unpacking My Library," which is reprinted in the first volume, inspired the title. Benjamin viewed the library as a repository of memories, and a world ready to be (re)discovered. He narrates his personal friendship with each of his books while unpacking them from a trunk: "Every passion borders on the chaotic, but the collector's passion borders on the chaos of memories." In the present volume Marcel Proust's excerpted essay, "On Reading," conjures up blissful memories of childhood reading, when time spent with a good book is like having a good friend.

Carrie Mae Weems agrees: "Books are my playmates, my best friends, my running buddies, my partners in crime, my solace, and my occasional lover." In *Writers and Their Books*, they are Junot Diaz's lifeline: "Books for me are many things: they are friends, they are companions, they are mentors, they are warnings, they clown; they entertain, they hearten, and they make me stronger. But most of all books (I say again and again) are like the Thirty-Mile Woman from Toni Morrison's *Beloved*: 'She is a friend of my mind. She gather me, man. The pieces I am, she father them and give them back to me in all the right order.'" Billie Tsien, architect for the Obama Presidential Center (and library), admits to being obsessed in *Architects and Their Books*: "I am a wanton reader—as long as it is fiction. In many ways it is an addiction because I always need to have my backup book and a backup of my backup." Flaubert had similar and more titillating advice: "The one way of tolerating existence is to lose oneself in literature as in a perpetual orgy."

The past ten years have seen a transformation in the culture of the book brought on by technological change, but adoption of e-readers and e-books has plateaued, and book lovers today might ask themselves if they could ever love a digital book.

"The simple act of flipping pages like it's a finger event has always been fulfilling, even if to just smell the pages," says Ed Ruscha. Carrie Mae Weems "is used to working with certain kinds of textures that resonate with the quality of words and pictures in a certain kind of way." For Theaster Gates, "there is the pleasure of touch . . . ; the ability to reach in and pull a thing out of its carton, to smell it. All of that other sensorial activity is very important to me and actually helps me read better, see better, memorize better, and understand an object better."

The death of the book has been bandied about for some time, but could we now be on the precipice of a new Dark Age—or, as author Matthew Battles terms the burning of the Great Library of Alexandria in *Libraries: An Unquiet History*, a "biblioclasm"? As Ray Bradbury reminds us, "You don't have to burn books to destroy a culture. Just get people to stop reading them." Public libraries have decommissioned tens of millions of printed books as they struggle with an identity crisis brought on by the digital era; but we may have reached a turning point. Printed books offer a tangible, powerful, and meaningful experience, and "reading" may simply continue to mean what it has meant for the last several hundred years. As Italian novelist, literary critic, philosopher, and semiotician Umberto Eco put it, "The book is like the spoon, scissors, the hammer, the wheel. Once invented, it cannot be improved."

Contemporary artists have taken up the bookshelf as a subject of exploration. Photographer Max-Steven Grossman and printmaker Phil Shaw create trompe l'oeil libraries (in a dust-free alternative to the bookshelf) to engage viewers in a personal dialogue with the images. Sean Landers's library canvases depict shelves of book spines comprising a continuous text that relates various fables connected to his work. In *Sorted Books*, conceptual artist Nina Katchadourian sorts book collections and stacks groups of books, top to bottom, to create book-spine poetry. Kerry James Marshall's painting *SOB, SOB* addresses the accumulation and dissemination of knowledge, depicting a bookshelf that reflects a thirst for information. Each work explores the materiality of the book, book collecting, and the act of reading.

Unpacking My Library celebrates notable personal libraries. "A library…is a life raft and a festival. They are cathedrals of the mind; hospitals of the soul; theme parks of the imagination," riffs British writer Caitlin Moran. Theaster Gates's library has the aged patina of a well-loved home, with its bulwarked shelves so sturdy that they seem capable of bearing the weight of a civilization. Janet Cardiff and George Bures Miller's doorstop of a Holy Bible sits between a blue mannequin head and a metronome. Billy Childish, who presents himself like a rakish professor, claims, "It's not a crazy idea to judge someone by their library"; browsing his shelves, I find myself wondering about the juxtaposition of Tracey Emin's *The Last Great Adventure Is You* and Childish's own *Frozen Estuary,* considering that Emin and Childish were once lovers. Mark Dion asks, "Does a library need to be only the books?" His wonderfully arcane collection is like a living encyclopedia, with titles like *Jelly Moulds, The Posthuman Dada Guide, Things Organized Neatly* (two copies), and *Never Give a Lady a Restive Horse* alongside archives and binders labeled "Persons of Great Interest," "Playful Images," and "Nurse." Tracey Emin's *Woody Guthrie Artworks* (2005) is a surprise; Guthrie was arguably Bob Dylan's greatest early influence. Wangechi Mutu's *Amazing Grace,* by Steve Turner, stands out in light of Carrie Mae Weems's *Grace Notes* project, inspired by President Barack Obama's singing of the hymn to honor a victim of Charleston's Emanuel African Methodist Episcopal Church shootings. Martin Parr points out that he has "a whole section of books that are sort of weird." (Umberto Eco, who had a library of 50,000 books, also counted among his books a collection devoted to wrongheadedness and stupidity.)

Theaster Gates speaks wistfully of the unread books on his shelves: "There is probably no way that I will read every book that I now have in my collection, but it gives me just endless pleasure attempting to." But could the unread books on our shelves be more valuable than the books we *have* read? "There is always at least a 100-book margin between what I own and what I've read," says Junot Diaz in *Writers and Their Books*. The great Italian prose writer and fabulist Italo Calvino wrote about classic books and building a personal library, "There is nothing for it but for all of us to invent our own ideal libraries of classics. I would say that such a library ought to be composed half of books we have read and that have really counted for us, and half of books we propose to read and presume will come to count—leaving a section of empty shelves for surprises and occasional discoveries."

Can books serve as a medium through which to understand more about an artist's life and work? Fyodor Dostoyevsky, Marcel Duchamp, Toni Morrison, James Baldwin, Henri Cartier-Bresson, Robert Frank, and Samuel Beckett all make appearances on artists' shelves and top-ten lists, but the big revelation is the prevalence of Dee Brown's *Bury My Heart at Wounded Knee: An Indian History of the American West*, its power to evoke empathy attested to by Mark Dion: "*Bury My Heart at Wounded Knee* was a landmark book for me… opening a melancholy place in me that never closed."

My hope is that readers will make a "finger event" of thumbing through these pages—and find a book worthy of a permanent place on their bookshelves.

—Jo Steffens

On Reading

Marcel Proust
Edited and translated by Damion Searls

There are perhaps no days of our childhood that we lived as fully as the days we think we left behind without living at all: the days we spent with a favorite book. Everything that filled others' days, so it seems, but that we avoided as vulgar impediments to a sacred pleasure—the game for whose sake a friend came looking for us right at the most interesting paragraph; the bothersome bee or sunbeam that forced us to look up from the book, or change position; the treats we had been forced to bring along but that we left untouched on the bench next to us while above our head the sun grew weaker in the blue sky; the dinner we had to go home for, during which we had no thought except to escape upstairs and finish, as soon as we were done, the interrupted chapter—our reading should have kept us from perceiving all that as anything other than obtrusive demands, but on the contrary, it has graven into us such happy memories of these things (memories much more valuable to us now than what we were reading with such passion at the time) that if, today, we happen to leaf through the pages of these books of the past, it is only because they are the sole calendars we have left of those bygone days, and we turn their pages in the hope of seeing reflected there the houses and lakes which are no more.

Who does not remember, as I do, this vacation-time reading that you tried to tuck away into one hour of the day after another, into every moment peaceful and inviolable enough to give it refuge. In the morning, after coming back from the park, when everyone had left "to go for a stroll," I would slip into the dining room where, until lunch, still such a long time away, no one would come in except for old Félicie, who was relatively quiet, and where my only companions, very considerate of my reading, were the painted plates hung with hooks on the wall, the calendar whose previous day's page had just been torn off, and the grandfather clock and the fire, both of which talked without asking you to answer them, and whose gentle speech, empty of meaning, never replaced, as people's words do, the meaning of the word you were reading.

———

I had not been reading in my room a very long time when I had to go out to the park, about half a mile from the village. But after the game I was forced to play, I would cut short my tasting of the treats that had been carried out in baskets and handed out to the children alongside the river, on the grass where the book had been put down with orders not to pick it up again. A little farther on, in certain of the park's rather wild and mysterious depths, the river ceased to be a rectilinear and artificial body of water bedecked with swans and bordered by paths where statues stood smiling, and instead rushed onward, now jumping with carp, at high speed past the park fence and turned into a river in the geographical sense of the word—a river deserving a name—before quickly flowing out (was it really the same water as the water between the statues, beneath the swans?) into the pastures where cattle lay sleeping, where it inundated the golden buttercups: a kind of meadow which the river turned marshy and which was joined to the village on one side by the crude towers that were left over, it was said, from the Middle Ages, and was joined to "nature" on the other side by means of the ascending paths of wild rose and hawthorn trees—a "nature" extending to infinity, to villages bearing other names, to the unknown. I would let the others finish eating down in the park, by the swans, and run up into the maze, to a bower where I could sit and not be found, with my back to the clipped hazelnut tree, and from there I could see the asparagus plants, the fringes of strawberry bushes, the pond into which, on some days, horses hitched to a wheel would pump water, the white gate up higher that was "the end of the park," and beyond it the fields of cornflower and poppy. In this bower the silence was deep and the risk of being discovered almost nonexistent, a safety rendered even sweeter by the distant cries down below, calling me in vain, sometimes even approaching, climbing the lower slopes, searching everywhere, before going back down, not having found what they were looking for; then no other sound; only, from time to time, the golden sound of the bells that, far away across the pastures, seemed to toll behind the blue sky and might have warned me of the passing hours, but I, surprised by how soft they sounded and disturbed by the deeper silence that followed after their last chimes had been emptied out of it, was never sure what time it had tolled. These were not the thundering bells that you heard when you returned to the village—when you neared the church that, from close up, regained its great, rigid height, its slate-gray cowl dotted with black crows rearing up into the evening blue—letting fly their bursts of sound across the square "for the bounties of the earth." These bells reached the park only weakly, softly, and addressed themselves not to me but to the whole countryside, all the villages, all the lonely farmers in their fields; they in no way compelled me to raise my head, they passed close by me, bearing the time of day into the distant countryside, without noticing me, without recognizing me, and without disturbing me.

And sometimes, at home, in my bed, long after dinner, the last hours of the evening also sheltered my reading, but only on the days when I had reached the final chapters of a book, when there was not much more to read to get to the end. Then, risking both punishment if I was discovered and

the insomnia that, once I had finished the book, might last all night, I re-lit my candle after my parents went to bed; in the street outside, between the gunsmith's house and the post office, bathed in silence, the sky was dark but nonetheless blue and full of stars, and to the left, on the raised lane just at the turn where its elevated ascent began, you could feel watching you the monstrous black apse of the church whose sculptures did not sleep at night—just a village church but still of historical importance, the magical abode of the Lord, of the consecrated bread, of multicolored saints, and of the ladies from the neighboring chateaux who, on feast days, making the hens squawk and the gossips stare, crossed the marketplace in their "turn-out" to go to mass and, on their way back, after leaving the shadow of the porch where the faithful, pushing open the vestibule door, scattered the errant rubies of the nave, did not pass the pastry shop on the square without buying one of those cakes in the shape of a tower, protected from the sun by an awning—"manqués," "Saint-Honorés," "Genoese"— cakes whose leisurely, sugary scent remains mixed in my mind with the bells of high mass and the happiness of Sundays.

When the last page had been read, the book was finished. With a deep sigh I had to halt the frantic racing of my eyes and of my voice, which had followed after my eyes without making a sound, stopping only to catch its breath. Then, to give the turmoil within me (unleashed too long to be able to calm down on its own) other movements to occupy itself with, I would stand up and walk back and forth next to my bed, my eyes still fixed on a point which one would have sought in vain within the room, or outside the room either, for it was located at a distance of the soul and nowhere else—one of those distances that cannot be measured in feet or miles like other distances, and that moreover it is impossible to confuse with the other kind of distance when you look at the "faraway" eyes of someone whose thoughts are "elsewhere." And now what? Is that all there was to the book? These beings to whom we had given more of our attention and affection than we give to the people in our life, not always daring to admit the extent to which we loved them, so that we even feigned boredom or closed the book with pretended indifference when our parents came upon us while we were reading and seemed to smile at our emotion; these people for whom we had panted and sobbed—we would never see them again, never learn anything more about them. Already, for a few pages in a cruel "Epilogue," the author had taken care to "trail off," leaving more and more space between the characters with an indifference simply unbelievable to anyone who knew the interest with which he had followed them, step by step, until that point. What these people did with every hour of their lives was told to us and then, suddenly: "Twenty years after these events, you might have met an old man on the streets of Fougères, his back not yet bent by age…" Having spent two volumes letting us glimpse the delightful possibilities of a certain marriage, having frightened us and then delighted us with every obstacle encountered and then overcome, the author let us learn from a passing comment by a secondary character that the marriage had taken place, we don't know exactly when or how—this astonishing epilogue seemed to have been written from the heights of heaven by someone who cared nothing for our transient passions, someone substituted somehow for our author. How we wanted the book to keep going, and, if that were not possible, wanted more information about all of its characters, wanted to learn something further about their lives, and spend our own on matters not altogether foreign to the love that they inspired within us, whose object we had suddenly lost; how we wanted not to have loved in vain, for an hour, those beings who tomorrow will be nothing but names on a forgotten page, in a book that has nothing to do with life, and whose value we had seriously mistaken, since its fate here below, we now understand (and our parents inform us, if necessary, with a contemptuous word), was not in the least to contain the whole of the world and all of destiny, as we had thought, but simply to occupy a very narrow place on a notary's bookshelf, between the undistinguished annals of the *Illustrated Magazine of Fashion* and the *Geography of the Eure-et-Loir Region*…

———

There is no doubt that friendship, friendship for individuals, is a frivolous thing, and reading is a friendship. But at least it is a sincere form of friendship, and the fact that it is directed at someone dead, someone absent, gives it something disinterested, almost touching. It is also a form of friendship unencumbered with everything that makes other friendships ugly. Since we all, we the living, are nothing but the dead who have not yet taken up our offices, all the courtesies, all the greetings in the entrance-hall, that we call respect, gratitude, and devotion and into which we mix so many lies, are unproductive and exhausting. Furthermore, from our first bonds of sympathy, admiration, and recognition, the first words we speak and the first letters we write weave around us the first threads of a web of habit, a veritable mode of existence which we can no longer extricate ourselves from in the ensuing friendships; not to mention that the excessive words we utter during this time remain, like promissory notes we have to pay, or else we will pay far more, for the rest of our lives, in self-reproach for having refused to honor them. In reading, friendship is suddenly returned to its initial purity. With books there is no civility. If we spend the evening with these friends, it is because we truly want to. From them, at least, we often part only with reluctance. And with none of the thoughts, when we have left them, that spoil other friendships: What did they think of us? Were we impolite? Did they like us? And the fear of being forgotten for someone else. All of these turmoils of friendship come to an end at the threshold of the pure and calm friendship of reading. No respectful deference either: we laugh at what Molière says only to the precise extent to which we find it funny; when he bores us we are not afraid to look bored; and when we have definitely had enough of him we put him back on the shelf as abruptly as if he were not a famous genius. The atmosphere of this pure form of friendship is a silence purer than words. For we speak for others, but keep silent for ourselves. Silence, too, does not carry the trace of our flaws, our hypocrisies, as words do. It is pure, it is an atmosphere in the truest sense. It does not interpose between the author's thought and our own the unavoidable obstacle, resistant to thought, of our different egos. Even the language of the book is pure (in any book worthy of the name), rendered transparent by the author's thought which has removed from the book everything that is not itself until the book becomes its faithful portrait; every sentence, fundamentally, is like every other, because they have all been spoken with the unique inflection of a single personality; there is thus a kind of continuity, incompatible with the interactions we have in life and with everything foreign to thought that those interactions mix into it, a continuity which instantly enables us to follow the true line of the author's thought, the features of his physiognomy, as reflected in this tranquil mirror. We can delight in one feature after another of each of these authors without needing them to be worthy, because it is a great spiritual pleasure to discern these profound depictions and to love them, in a friendship without ego, without fine phrases, as if inside ourselves.

Artists and Their Books

Janet Cardiff and George Bures Miller

An Interview
with Janet Cardiff

JO STEFFENS: Your 2008 installation *The House of Books Has No Windows* was built using five thousand antique books. Can you talk about what motivated you to create this piece, which you describe as "Spines out, pages in, the work is a library turned in on itself, a space of infinite possibility where nothing may be read yet everything imagined"?

JANET CARDIFF: When you go inside *The House of Books,* there is such silence and a certain smell of old books, but at the same time you are surrounded by all of these complete virtual worlds that expand outward. There are so many levels of metaphor at work in it… the house as a repository of stories, or the dark interior space, like our own minds, with its layers of stories. Another analogy would be how the sculpture of books becomes a miniature Internet-like web, with so many different complex stories surrounding the viewer.

Several of our works use the concept that books are like portals into virtual worlds. Another is *The Dark Pool,* an installation that has layers of old books in it.

Can you tell us about the books you selected for your top-ten list, or maybe pick a couple to talk about? If you could add one more book to the list, what would it be?

I don't know how I can talk about just a couple… I love all of these books so much. But I will try to be brief and pick a few. The books of Emily Carr: I love her simple stories from her childhood through to her older age as a struggling poor female artist…. In the early 1900s she lived with her dogs and her pet rat and her multiple board-ers, who provided her with an income to keep painting. *Labyrinths* and *Ubik* are two books that I go back to every few years to reread. I'm very attracted to their inventive alternative views of reality that are so filmic and visual. *The Lady in the Car with Glasses and a Gun* is really a mind puzzle in the detective genre. With [Sébastien] Japrisot you never are quite sure what is going on. I think he is very much connected to French New Wave writers like [Alain] Robbe-Grillet (*The Erasers*), in that even the protagonist gets confused about what is reality. I can't add just

one more book… others that I considered were *Snowcrash* by Neal Stephenson, *Extremely Loud and Incredibly Close* by Jonathan Safran Foer, *Lit* by Mary Karr, *What Is the What* by Dave Eggers, *The Sisters Brothers* by Patrick deWitt, and *Three Day Road* by Joseph Boyden.

What is the role of literature in your life; is it as important as art history, and what does it mean for your art practice?

Literature is more important than art history for my art practice. When you are reading, your brain is relaxed but also going off on tangents caused by what you are reading. Sometimes I realize that I've read two pages without taking anything in because I've still been thinking about something from an earlier page. Reading for pleasure is for me a very stimulating aesthetic experience and gives me a lot of ideas.

Do you have books on your shelves that you hope to read, or know you will never read; or do you typically read just about every book you own?

There are many books that I haven't read on the shelves. Unread books suggest another lifestyle … one in which I have time to just sit and read for weeks. Most often the books that I reread are classic mysteries like those by Chandler, Hammett, or Japrisot. Several of the books on my list I have read a couple of times, like the stories of Emily Carr and Borges. I like to reread these because I'm always changing in what I'm thinking about so that the books and stories become quite new to me and give me new ideas.

Do you ever feel like you have too many books? Is there one book not in your library that you wish you owned?

Sometimes I feel that I have too many books … I'd like to cull the library, but George doesn't ever want to part with books, so we just keep stuffing more on the shelves. I don't really covet any books, although some original Emily Carr sketchbook stories would be a dream, but those are better to leave in the museums.

How do you decide which books to read and buy? Do you visit bookstores to browse the shelves and to serendipitously discover new books?

Usually finding books to read is a serendipitous experience or a recommendation from someone. I started reading *The Diving Bell and the Butterfly* by Jean-Dominique Bauby, which I didn't know we owned but which I found on our bookshelf by chance. At the same time I had been reading about Joan Didion in the *Atlantic,* so I signed out her *Blue Nights* from the library. Near the end of *Blue Nights* Didion talks about Bauby's book … that gave me the shivers, because I had just finished it.

Where do you prefer to read — in a comfortable chair, at a desk, or in bed? Do you keep notes in the margins, turn down pages, mark or annotate pages in any other way?

Like many people I'm pretty busy, so I read in bits … before I sleep at night in bed or in the morning in an easy chair looking out at our river view. Beautiful landscape and book reading go together.

In the studio I have many art books that I read. Also sometimes in the evenings I sit in front of a fire, reading... lately it's a book called *The Japanese Mind,* by Roger J. Davies. The only books that I tend to read right through, and during the day, are detective novels—I have to be careful about how often I start one of those, because that becomes very time-consuming.

Do you read for pleasure, out of curiosity, or professionally? Are there certain books that have helped you in your own work?

I read for all of those reasons. I never know what will stimulate my artwork. One book that recently gave me an idea for a piece was a short story in *Snapshots* by Alain Robbe-Grillet.

Given the wide range of books in your library and on your top-ten list, would you say that making art requires a mix of influences and a broad knowledge of culture? Do you learn from other disciplines?

For me art making requires brain stimulation.... I like to read a wide range of books or magazines... science or film theory, essays... contemporary ideas, but art theory or philosophy usually puts me to sleep. I like the stimulation of traveling to different cities and museums, but at the same time, living in almost cultural isolation in our rural environment gives my mind the silence and boredom that is essential for my creativity.

Is there one book that stands out as having had a huge impact on you when you first read it?

When I was young, *Bury My Heart at Wounded Knee* was a powerful book for me. *Labyrinths* by Jorge Luis Borges and his stories in *The Garden of Forking Paths* or *The Library of Babel* really hit me; also influential were *La Jetée* by Chris Marker and *The Film Sense* by Serge Eisenstein.

Are there works of fiction that helped you navigate young adulthood?

For some reason I was very interested in Jewish writers in my formative teen years and I read a lot of Chaim Potok and Elie Weisel. I also had the same English teacher as Alice Munro. Not only was she a great teacher, but she also introduced me to Canadian literature with books by Sinclair Ross (*The Painted Door*), Margaret Laurence (*The Diviners*), and Robertson Davies (*The Deptford Trilogy*), and of course *Lives of Girls and Women* by Munro. This particular book was very influential for me in that Munro's potent emotional scenes, set in the same small town, really stuck in my mind. At university I started to read the classics, like Thomas Hardy and [Fyodor] Dostoyevsky, who both had a big effect on me—they made me so frustrated with their characters' inability to control their lives that I felt more control over my own.

At what age did you begin to seek out books? Did you use the library when you were young?

I went to a one-room country school for grades 2 and 3.… The small school had eight grades and one teacher, so you had to be quite independent in your learning. The library there had only a few hundred books. I remember my love of reading starting there, with historical fiction like *The Sword in the Stone* and the *Little House on the Prairie*. I remember sitting at the old-style desk, reading at recess.

**Top Ten Books
Janet Cardiff**

Patti Smith, *Just Kids*

Bernie Krause,
*The Great Animal
Orchestra*

Michael Ondaatje,
*The Collected Works
of Billy the Kid*

Emily Carr, *The
Book of Small*

Jorge Luis Borges,
Labyrinths

Philip K. Dick, *Ubik*

Sébastien Japrisot,
*The Lady in the
Car with Glasses
and a Gun*

Alice Munro, *Lives
of Girls and Women*

Leonard Shlain,
*Art & Physics:
Parallel Visions
in Space, Time
and Light*

W. G. Sebald,
Austerlitz

THE SUNDAY TIMES BESTSELLER

JUST KIDS

PATTI SMITH

The
GREAT ANIMAL
ORCHESTRA

Finding the Origins
of Music
in the World's Wild Places

BERNIE KRAUSE

THE
COLLECTED
WORKS OF
BILLY
THE KID

by MICHAEL
ONDAATJE

Anansi

EMILY CARR

THE BOOK
OF SMALL

INTRODUCTION BY SARAH ELLIS

LABYRINTHS
Selected Stories & Other Writings
BY JORGE LUIS BORGES

HUGO AWARD NOVELIST
PHILIP K. DICK
UBIK

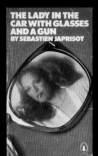

THE LADY IN THE
CAR WITH GLASSES
AND A GUN
BY SEBASTIEN JAPRISOT

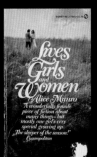

Lives
of Girls
and
Women
Alice Munro

"A wonderfully female
piece of fiction about
many things — but
mostly one girl's very
special growing up.
The sleeper of the season."
Cosmopolitan

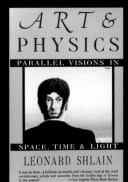

ART &
PHYSICS
PARALLEL VISIONS IN

SPACE, TIME & LIGHT
LEONARD SHLAIN

"A tour de force... A brilliant, accessible, and visionary look at the most
revolutionary artists and scientists from the Golden Age of Greece
to the present." —Los Angeles Times Book Review

AUSTERLITZ
W. G. SEBALD

JO STEFFENS: How old were you when you began to read on your own? Did you visit the library?

GEORGE BURES MILLER: I guess I was five or six. The library in my hometown was just a dusty room in the basement of an old brick building. There was very little space, and the stacks were way too close together and too high for me to reach everything.… I loved wandering in this maze of books and was amazed at how such a small room could hold so many places, ideas, and stories. No other library has quite fired my imagination the way that one did, and I remember my disappointment when they closed and moved to a new building.

Are there works of fiction that helped you navigate through young adulthood? Were there heroes or heroines that you identified with?

Raymond Chandler's Philip Marlowe, and L. M. Montgomery's Anne Shirley—two totally different characters in two totally different environments.

Is there one book that stands out as having had a huge impact on you when you first read it?

When I read *Slaughterhouse-Five* in high school, its antiwar message seemed so relevant, but I was also amazed at how Vonnegut could combine an emotional, historical narrative with an experimental science-fiction one.

Do you think the experience of viewing one of your multichannel environments is similar to the feeling of being absorbed by a good book? Your beautifully crafted installations are self-contained worlds unto themselves.

I guess the effect of a work like *The Murder of Crows* is similar to that of a book. The audience sits, surrounded by ninety-eight speakers, and the only visuals provided are through sound effects and Janet's voice. Often they sit with their eyes closed, imagining the worlds that we are trying to create through only words and sound. In other works, such as the video walks, we lean more toward a filmic immersion, where the reality of the physical space overlaps with that of the fictional space.

**Top Ten Books
George Bures Miller**

Jane Austen, *Pride and Prejudice*

L. M. Montgomery, *Anne of Green Gables*

Jack London, *South Sea Tales*

Hugh Lofting, *The Voyages of Doctor Dolittle*

Raymond Chandler, *Farewell, My Lovely*

Philip K. Dick, *The Man in the High Castle*

Kurt Vonnegut, *Slaughterhouse-Five*

Margaret Atwood, *The Edible Woman*

Margaret Laurence, *The Diviners*

William Gibson, *Neuromancer*

Pride & Prejudice

ANNE of GREEN GABLES
L. M. MONTGOMERY

SOUTH SEA TALES

Jack LONDON

THE VOYAGES OF DOCTOR DOLITTLE
HUGH LOFTING

RAYMOND CHANDLER
FAREWELL, MY LOVELY

Berkley Science Fiction

THE MAN IN THE HIGH CASTLE
Philip K. Dick

SLAUGHTERHOUSE-FIVE
OR
The Children's Crusade
A NEW NOVEL BY
KURT VONNEGUT, JR.

MARGARET ATWOOD
A NOVEL
THE EDIBLE WOMAN

Margaret Laurence
A Novel
The Diviners

NEUROMANCER
WILLIAM GIBSON

Melvin Van Peebles
Presents

The Harlem Cycle Vol I

A Rage in Harlem

The Real Cool Killers

The Crazy Kill

CHESTER HIMES

PAYBACK PRESS

RAYMOND CHANDLER
THE SIMPLE ART OF MURDER

RAYMOND CHANDLER
KILLER IN THE RAIN

RAYMOND CHANDLER
FAREWELL, MY LOVELY

THE BIG SLEEP
Raymond Chandler

And Then There Were None
Agatha Christie

MICHAEL CRICHTON
CONGO

AGATHA CHRISTIE

DEATH COMES AS THE END
GROSSET & DUNLAP

JAMES ELLROY

THE BLACK DAHLIA

NIGHTFALL
THE CASE OF THE COUNTERFEIT EYE
David Goodis
BLACK LIZARD BOOKS

SHOOT THE PIANO PLAYER
David Goodis
BLACK LIZARD

BLACK FRIDAY
David Goodis
BLACK LIZARD BOOKS

DAVID GOODIS
THE MOON IN THE GUTTER

DARK PASSAGE
David GOODIS
PRION

The Big Knockover
Dashiell Hammett
V-829 VINTAGE

DASHIELL HAMMETT THE THIN MAN
V-774 Vintage

DASHIELL HAMMETT **THE GLASS KEY**
V-773 Vintage

Sebastien Japrisot
The Lady in the Car with Glasses and a Gun

Sebastien Japrisot
Trap for Cinderella

Sebastien Japrisot
The Sleeping-Car Murders

NICOLAS FREELING
BECAUSE OF THE CATS

Elmore Leonard **THE HOT KID**

JOHN LE CARRE
CALL FOR THE DEAD

Sol

TONY HILLERMAN — TALKING GOD

TINKER TAILOR SOLDIER SPY · JOHN LE CARRÉ

P. D. JAMES · UNNATURAL CAUSES

P. D. JAMES · DEVICES AND DESIRES · A COLLINS MYSTERY

THE FUGITIVE EYE · CHARLOTTE JAY

BARRY MAITLAND · THE MARX SISTERS · ORION

BRIAN MOORE · COLD HEAVEN · PENGUIN

malko: SPYMASTER · DEATH IN SANTIAGO · de Villiers · ISBN 0-503-00883-X

A PURPLE PLACE FOR DYING · John D. MacDonald

THE NO. 1 LADIES' DETECTIVE AGENCY · ALEXANDER McCALL SMITH

LUDLUM · THE BOURNE IDENTITY · GRANADA

ELLIS PETERS · A MORBID TASTE FOR BONES · WARNER FUTURA

Ellis Peters · The Virgin in the Ice

The Disposables · Andrew J. Peterson

SARA PARETSKY · TUNNEL VISION · The New York Times Bestseller

Ian Rankin · A Good Hanging · ORION

TURN ON THE HEAT · A. A. FAIR (Erle Stanley Gardner)

THE CASE OF THE SHAPELY SHADOW · Jim Thompson · Black Lizard / CREATIVE ARTS

POP. 1280 · Jim Thompson · BLACK LIZARD BOOKS

THE CRIMINAL · Jim Thompson · BLACK LIZARD / CREATIVE ARTS

A SWELL-LOOKING BABE · Jim Thompson · Black Lizard / CREATIVE ARTS

A HELL OF A WOMAN

THE DUTCH SHOE MYSTERY · ELLERY QUEEN

MADMAN · WINCHESTER

Detective

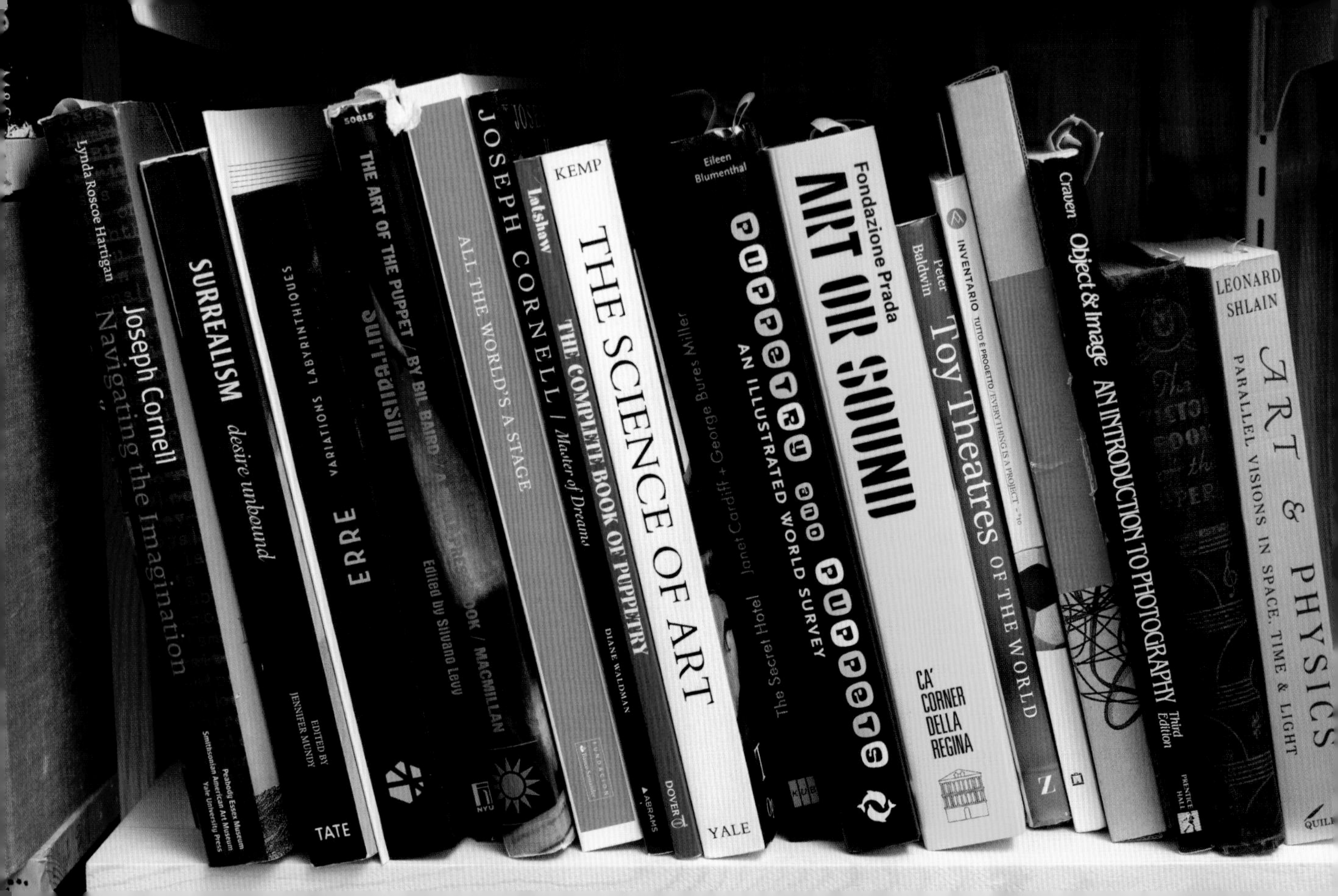

Lynda Roscoe Hartigan
Joseph Cornell
Navigating the Imagination
Peabody Essex Museum
Smithsonian American Art Museum
Yale University Press
SURREALISM desire unbound
EDITED BY JENNIFER MUNDY
TATE
VARIATIONS LABYRINTHIQUES
ERRE
THE ART OF THE PUPPET / BY BIL BAIRD
MACMILLAN
Edited by Silvano Levy
ALL THE WORLD'S A STAGE
JOSEPH CORNELL / Master of Dreams
DIANE WALDMAN
ABRAMS
Latshaw
THE COMPLETE BOOK OF PUPPETRY
DOVER
KEMP
THE SCIENCE OF ART
YALE
Janet Cardiff + George Bures Miller
The Secret Hotel
Eileen Blumenthal
PUPPETRY AND PUPPETS
AN ILLUSTRATED WORLD SURVEY
Fondazione Prada
ART OR SOUND
CA' CORNER DELLA REGINA
Peter Baldwin
Toy Theatres OF THE WORLD
INVENTARIO
TUTTO È PROGETTO / EVERYTHING IS A PROJECT
Craven
Object & Image
AN INTRODUCTION TO PHOTOGRAPHY
Third Edition
PRENTICE HALL
LEONARD SHLAIN
ART & PHYSICS
PARALLEL VISIONS IN SPACE, TIME & LIGHT
QUILL

Edward Rutherfurd   LONDON

CAROL SHIELDS   THE COLLECTED STORIES   VINTAGE CANADA

ERIC SIBLIN   THE CELLO SUITES   J.S. Bach, Pablo Casals, and the Search for a Baroque Masterpiece   ANANSI

33 MOMENTS OF HAPPINESS   Ingo Schulze   VINTAGE

NEW LIVES   Ingo Schulze   Vintage

OLIVER SACKS   AN ANTHROPOLOGIST ON MARS   KNOPF CANADA

AUSTERLITZ   W. G. SEBALD   Penguin

Granta   Iain Sinclair · Lights Out for the Territory

One Day in the Life of Ivan Denisovich   Alexander Solzhenitsyn

Story of O   by Pauline Réage

EXTREMELY LOUD & INCREDIBLY CLOSE   JONATHAN SAFRAN FOER

EVERYTHING IS ILLUMINATED   JONATHAN SAFRAN FOER

FRANKENSTEIN   Mary Shelley

JUST KIDS   PATTI SMITH

DARK WATER   KOJI SUZUKI   VERTICAL.

TOLS...   WAR AND PEACE   CARLTON HOU...

Billy Childish

MATTHIAS NEUMANN: Do you consider yourself a collector?

BILLY CHILDISH: Not really. I try not to be a collector of anything. I tend to get quite a few books, and quite a few hats, and I have quite a few guitars. I have always tried not to collect records. I am not one of these people who searches for things or has to go into a bookstore or record store, probably because I might start collecting things and I don't want to. Because I don't want to have any added insanity with collecting. I find life cluttered enough without encouraging it.

Do books as objects matter to you?

Yes. I used to run a small press. I started making fanzines in '77, and gradually it turned into book making, making both paperbacks and hardcover books. I either like high-end or low-end quality. I hate middle-quality. I have done printing myself, and I really do like letterpress. I guess I appreciate the aesthetic of things, and I am really into the material and what things are made out of.

When I used to run my small press, Hangman Books, there was this huge range of cards and colors to make really good wood-free books on a small scale. Ideally I would still do letterpress, and books would be properly made. I like it when people care about what they do and something isn't just a disposable object.

Have you ever discarded books or given them away?

What I've done over the years is that I always get rid of books that I think I can do without, and can possibly replace, unless they're books that I will reread again. So every few years I have a grooming of my library, but it still has left me with an awful lot of books. I recently moved house, and at the moment it is probably as sorted out as it has ever been, but already I do not have enough room and so they get stacked on top of each other. I have never really called it my library, it's just a bunch of bookcases, and there are a few of them.

You work as a musician, writer, publisher, and painter; do you consider each discipline separately, or as a multi- or interdisciplinary artist?

I just don't like it to be a prop to stand behind something. I like it to stand on its own. Of course it can inform the other things. And I used to even use different names in different areas to try not to overidentify with my persona as an artist in any of them. I like for things to have their own life and their own standing. When I was published by Virgin and then went to Random House, they placed me in the counterculture section. And I said, "Well, why can't it just be in another section"? I don't see why anybody wants to willingly go into a ghetto of any description. I think the whole thing should be flat. We don't need the problem of another identity. You already have the problem with the one already, without adding another one.

What books do you use as reference material in your studio?

I am a great admirer of Munch's work, and a friend brought a catalog from the Munch and Van Gogh exhibition in Norway. I will very often leave a certain page open and imagine it will have some impact. Fortunately, or unfortunately—I am not sure which it is—that doesn't really happen, but it certainly gives me some kind of inspiration to have one or two pieces of art around or available that are acting otherworldly, and carry a charge which is valuable. It is a great thing to learn from the masters and choose who the masters are going to be. Not what is contemporary, not what is fashionable, but what actually and authentically you respond to.

The thing about Dostoyevsky; I found out that his translations in English were often dressed up, and that the original writing was a bit rougher and not quite up to standards. So they corrected him a little bit. I am always looking for this rough cut in music, in painting, and in writing. In writing I try to make it look like it's never been worked on, it's never been written by a writer. And in a way that would be true in the paintings, and in the music; bringing yourself in as neutral all the time.

My understanding of how you work is that it is somewhat a compulsion of doing, and not so much revisiting things. How does that translate into revisiting books and rereading certain books?

I actually do reread books quite a lot. And I would say subjects keep reoccurring, and are actually revisited quite often. For Robert Walser, writing a book was pretty much writing a book about himself every time. I am interested in the alchemy of how you do things, how you move from one place to another, like in a story. I am interested in other people's use of smoke and mirrors. And how my smoke and mirrors work. I don't have quiet reverence for artistic endeavors—in many ways, I think it is basically smoke and mirrors. You want to understand the trick that fools you, but you want to be fooled.

You have a sense of style in terms of being aware of how you present yourself to the world.

With my sense of style it is a dialogue with myself, not with the world, even if I am a bit dandified sometimes when I dress strangely. As far as writing goes, I didn't read until I was about fourteen, and I am quite seriously dyslexic, not having had the formal education, and not having read the books that other people read in school or university; so twenty years ago I read Kafka for the first time because I was put off by all the intellectual toddle about Kafka. The *Metamorphosis* was just a great laugh. I love that sort of play with things. Certain sections of Dostoyevsky are so current and so modern. If you look at present and timeless, the same thing happens with *Hunger*—apart from that every now and then he mentions the horse and carriage, you wouldn't know that it wasn't completely contemporary.

Can you talk about some of your favorite books?

I really like the first part of *Don Quixote*, but I don't like the second part that much; it's a bit poncey. I do like the *Iliad* a lot; I like all the repetition, and all the descriptions of how people died, and the lists of ships. I just love the insanity of that spoken-word tradition when this book came together, and you weren't allowed to leave anyone out who was involved in this event.

What are your thoughts on audiobooks?

One of my favorite documentaries was on the American Civil War. I think David McCullough does the voice-over, and it's a masterpiece in the way he delivers it. But you don't get many people with a measure of quality to their voice that makes it about the words. There is a fantastic bit in *Demons*, by Dostoyevsky, when supposedly the character is doing a reading based on the Russian author Turgenev. Dostoyevsky said that the thing that mattered to Turgenev when he was reading this story wasn't the tragedy, but that "I am here and I am telling you." I love that sort of insight, that perception and that understanding of the conceit of authors or painters or humans. There is nothing wrong with style, but there is nothing right with it either.

But that still might be different for different people.

You see, these writers and musicians and pop people, they are the false prophets we were warned about; these are the people attributed with mystical powers. You're in for a penny and a pound with fans, and we identify ourselves so much through what we like. I am an intellectual guy, I am a punk-rock guy, and I am whatever type of guy. It's tribal, and I don't want to be a member of the tribe, you pay through the nose for it.

Are you a tribe of one?

Oh no. My friends are dead Russians, dead painters, cave painters. You could say that many people's bookshelves could be their validation. It's not a crazy idea to judge someone by their library, but it's always a question of how many of the books you have actually read, and how many of them are just there for the decoration. It's really funny, because coming from a nonliterary background, I read all of Dostoyevsky, and I meet people from an academic background who have not read a word, but they have the books. The way I found out who to read was by someone telling me: why don't you read this. I read Dostoyevsky because I read Charles Bukowski.

Top Ten Books
Billy Childish

W. H. Auden,
Van Gogh:
A Self-Portrait

John Fante, *Wait*
until Spring, Bandini

Fyodor Dostoyevsky,
Demons

Knut Hamsun,
Hunger

Swami Dayananda,
The Teaching of
the Bhagavad Gita

Nikolai Gogol,
Diary of a Madman
and Other Stories

Robert Walser,
Institute Benjamenta

Daniil Kharms,
Incidences

Homer, *The Iliad*

Hans Fallada,
The Drinker

Vincent

WAIT
UNTIL
SPRING,
BANDINI

JOHN
FANTE

DEMONS

FYODOR DOSTOEVSKY

THE NEW TRANSLATION BY
RICHARD PEVEAR AND LARISSA VOLOKHONSKY

HUNGER

KNUT HAMSUN

The
teaching
of the
Bhagavad

SWAMI DAYANAN

PENGUIN CLASSICS

NIKOLAI GOGOL

DIARY OF A MADMAN
AND OTHER STORIES

INSTITVTE
BENJAMENTA

ROBERT WALSER

EXTRAORDINARY
CLASSICS

daniil

KHARMS

INCIDENCES

"Luminous fragments of the avant-garde." TLS

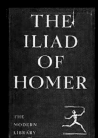

THE
ILIAD
OF
HOMER

THE
MODERN
LIBRARY

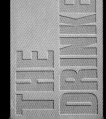

Hans Fallada

with an introduction
by John Willett

THE DRINKER

Van Gogh

VAN GOGH

FINLEY

cézanne

ROBERTS

100 Artists' Manifestos: From the Futurists to the Stuckists

BRAZILIAN POPULAR PRINTS

James Cauty

AHS PRACTICAL GUIDES

DRAWING DOGS · DIANA THORNE

A NEW CONCISE REFERENCE DICTIONARY

Neal Brown

KANDINSKY

CONCERNING THE SPIRITUAL IN ART

Baudelaire

THE MIRROR OF ART

DOVER ART LIBRARY

SMALL TREES

JAKE & DINOS CHAPMAN

FRANS MASEREEL

THE RAPE OF CREATIVITY

JOSEF HERMAN

MODERN ART OXFORD

EXORGIEN I-III SEXORGIES II

SEXORGIEN II SEXORGIES II

JOURNEYS

BILLY CHILDISH

TRACEY EMIN

THE LAST GREAT ADVENTURE IS YOU

FROZEN ESTUARY

WHITE CUBE

'13

billy childish

Los Angeles 2013

international art objects galleries / Koenig Books

billy childish

New York 2013

Lehmann Maupin / Koenig Books

billy childish

Berlin 2013

neugerriemschneider / Koenig Books

billy childish

walking in god's busi

HOW TO ATTAIN ENLIGHTENMENT — SWAMI

Qigong for Healing and Relaxation · Michael Tse

SCHULMAN · KARMIC ASTROLOGY · The Moon's Nodes & Reincarnation · Martin Schulman

Intuitive Awareness · Ajahn Sumedho

When buddhists living christ · LAMA SURYA DAS

Fremantle & Trungpa · THE TIBETAN BOOK OF THE DEAD · Shambhala

TRUNGPA · THE ESSENTIAL CHÖGYAM TRUNGPA · SHAMBHALA

LAURENCE G. BOLDT · THE TAO OF ABUNDANCE · EIGHT ANCIENT PRINCIPLES FOR ABUNDANT LIVING · PENGUIN ARKANA

SADHANA - A Way to God · Walking on Water · COLUMBA

Swartz · Mystic by Default · de Mello · SHININGWORLD PRESS

WHAT THE BUDDHA TAUGHT · WALPOLA RAHULA · GROVE PRESS

TRUNGPA · DHARMA ART · SHAMBHALA

THE PROMISED LAND

Gut and Psychology Syndrome · Dr. Rick Norris · Mediuform

CHÖGYAM TRUNGPA · THE PATH IS THE GOAL · A Basic Handbook of Buddhist Meditation · SHAMBHALA

THE WISDOM OF INSECURITY · Alan Watts · RIDER

EN190 · Venerable Ācariya Mun Bhūridatta Thera · A Spiritual Biography · by Acariya Mahā Boowa Ñāṇasampanno

THE PATHWORK OF SELF-TRANSFORMATION · EVA PIERRAKOS · BANTAM NEW AGE BOOKS

CHÖDRON · THE WISDOM OF NO ESCAPE · B

The Heart of the Buddha's Teaching · THICH NHAT HANH

Chögyam Trungpa · ORDERLY CHAOS · SHAMBHALA

Blistered Feet, Blissful Mind · by Tim Price · VIPASSANA MEDITATION · Venerable Sayadaw U Janakabhivamsa · HEAD BOOKS

ECKHART TOLLE · ~ PRACTICING THE POWER OF NOW ~

KARMA & REINCARNATION — DR HIROSHI MOTOYAMA

SADHANA A WAY TO GOD — ANTHONY DE MELLO

Trungpa · **THE MYTH OF FREEDOM**

TRUNGPA · NALANDA · **THE LIFE OF MARPA** THE TRANSLATOR

Venerable Father · *Freeing the Heart* ~ The Nuns' Community at Amaravati & Cittaviveka · Paul Breiter

— *The Way It Is* — · Ajahn Sumedho

The Chinese Art of TAI CHI CH'UAN

SUTTA-NIPĀTA · H Saddhatissa

Trungpa · **CUTTING THROUGH SPIRITUAL MATERIALISM**

Chögyam Trungpa · **TRANSCENDING MADNESS**

Chögyam Trungpa

The **WAY OF NON-ATTACHMENT** · DHIRAVAMSA

MOOR · NATURE'S HEALING MIRACLE · **The Power of Your Other Hand** · PETER J. HUDSON · CAPACCHIONE

CHODRON · **THE WISDOM OF NO ESCAPE**

CHOGYAM TRUNGPA · **THE PATH IS THE GOAL** · A Basic Handbook of Buddhist Meditation · SHAMBHALA

MANDALA · LAO TZU TAO TE CHING · **THE BOOK OF LIEH-TZU** · TRANSLATED BY A C GRAHAM

EUGEN HERRIGEL · **ZEN IN THE ART OF ARCHERY**

EKNATH EASWARAN · **THE DHAMMAPADA**

THE UPANISHADS

Chögyam Trungpa · **ILLUSION'S GAME** · Shambhala

Tao and Dharma CHINESE MEDICINE AND AYURVEDA · Robert Svoboda and Arnie Lade

TRUNGPA · **BORN IN TIBET** · SHAMBHALA

THE HEART OF UNDERSTANDING · THICH NHAT HANH · PARALLAX PRESS

ZWEIG

Beware of
PITY

R U

HER
PRIVATES
WE

DAVIES

HER PRIVATES WE · FREDERIC MANNING

Adventures
of a
Despatch
Rider

MAJOR
W.H.L.
WATSON

WILLIAM
BLACKWOOD
& SONS

THE
STORM OF
STEEL

*

JÜNGER

*

WITH INTRODUCTION
BY
R.H. MOTTRAM

*

CHATTO & WINDUS

HELL'S
CORNER
1940

H.R.P.
BOORMAN

KENT
MESSENGER

FIRE · ARMY · THE

1914 – DAY WAR — 1918

The Real Dad's Army · Norman Longmate

Old Soldiers Never Die
By FRANK RICHARDS

Faber
Q
Books

THE LIFE

THE LORE AND FOLK POETRY OF THE BLACK HUSTLER

By Dennis Wepman Ronald B. Newman Murray B. Binderman

GUILTY MEN by 'CATO'

3/6

Ernst Friedrich

Krieg dem Kriege

RIEL

The Strange Empire of Louis Riel

JOHN COULTER

2001 · 99714-5 DM

SWAN

99–104

MY HAPPY DAYS IN HELL

György Faludy

MODERN CLASSIC

HELMET FOR MY PILLOW

ROBERT LECKIE

SIX WEEKS

JOHN LEWIS-STEMPEL

WITH A MACHINE GUN TO CAMBRAI

GEORGE COPPARD

MARTIN MIDDLEBROOK THE FIRST DAY ON THE SOMME

Sapper Martin

EDITED AND INTRODUCED BY RICHARD VAN EMDEN

John Hersey Hiroshima

MODERN CLASSICS

THE ADVANCE FROM MONS

CAPTAIN WALTER BLOEM

T. 164

ON THE FRONT LINE

TRUE WORLD WAR I STORIES

FOREWORD BY MALCOLM BROWN

CONSTABLE

Witkop

GERMAN STUDENTS' WAR LETTERS

PEN & SWORD MILITARY CLASSICS

WITH THE GERMAN GUNS

HERBERT SULZBACH

LYN MACDONALD · 1914 · THE DAYS OF HOPE

ISBN 0-14-01157-6

The Sixth Grandfather

BLACK ELK SPEAKS — Neihardt

Tribal Peoples for Tomorrow's World

BURY MY HEART AT WOUNDED KNEE — DEE BROWN

THE INDIAN TIPI — BLACK ELK'S THE SACRED PIPE — Reginald and Gladys Laubin — Brown

Black Elk's Story — RICE

SHORT NIGHTS of the SHADOW CATCHER — TIMOTHY EGAN

HOLY BIBLE — Revised Standard Version — WITH HARDED COPYING PICTURES

ELAINE PAGELS — The Gospel of Thomas — MEYER

GOSPEL TRUTH — The New Image of Jesus Emerging from Science and History, and Why It Matters — RUSSELL SHORTO

THE ELK (WORLD) — THE JESUS SEMINAR — Macmillan

A PENNSYLVANIA GERMAN EMBLEM BOOK — THE PICTURE-BIBLE OF LUDWIG DENIG — YODER — I — III

A PENNSYLVANIA GERMAN EMBLEM BOOK — THE PICTURE-BIBLE OF LUDWIG DENIG — II — III

THE LOST GOSPEL — MACK — ELEMENT

Mark Dion

Mark Dion with
greyhound Hera

JO STEFFENS: Your library could be described as a treasure trove; do you curate the shelves, and can you give us a short tour?

MARK DION: It may be a treasure trove; however, I don't have glittering gold but I have the golden spines of vintage *National Geographic* magazines and a reprint of *The Golden Game* and issues of *The Yellow Book*. I may not have pearls but rather the ivory covers of *October*. I don't have emeralds and gems but the marvelous blues and greens of covers of the works of naturalist William Beebe. My books are not particularly organized except by size. In fact many of my books are mixed with those of my wife, Dana Sherwood. Cookbooks, historic works on etiquette, and anything by Edith Wharton or Virginia Woolf most likely will be Dana's books. There are some sections of the library that may feature old volumes by naturalists, or field guides, or my Dover books of pictorial reference, but most other parts are truly a chaotic mess. The literature is nestled beside art books, stacked with texts on ecology and history. Still I have pretty excellent recall as to what I have in the library and where it usually lives. I dream of a period of house arrest when I can take time to bring some order to this wilderness of volumes. As you perhaps observe from some of the photos, I also mix my most precious objects with the books. My collection of animal flash cards, my lead figures, finials, well-loved plush animals, plaster busts, plant and animal specimens and vernacular postcards. Does a library need to be only the books?

The ten books you highlight are shown chronologically, starting with when they first came into your life. Can you tell us more about them?

My deep love for books as objects as well as containers of knowledge derives from growing up in a house without them. During my life, I never witnessed either of my parents reading a book. Certainly my mother never read a book, and while my father claimed to have read during World War II, he never picked up a book in my lifetime. When I visited people's homes as a child and saw their books, I was totally fascinated and magnetically drawn to them. Eventually, through much begging, we acquired a *Golden Book Encyclopedia*, which could be obtained one volume each week at the grocery store. The only other book that I recall being at home was the *Golden Nature Guide to Seashores*. I devoured the book, and since we lived by the sea, I could immediately apply the knowledge between the covers. This is the book that lit the fuse for my lifelong love of field guides to natural places. The other books on the list mark touchstones in my education. *Bury My Heart at Wounded Knee* was a landmark book for me, introducing me to thinking critically about conventional history and media, and opening a melancholy place in me that never closed. Reading the work in my first year of high school marked a new skepticism in my outlook. Alexander Wilson's *The Culture of Nature* was such a valuable book in helping me articulate my concerns. He was the first writer I encountered who spoke with such concise and beautifully crafted words about ideas at the very core of my practice. It was such a catastrophe that he died so young. *Bouvard and Pécuchet* provided me with a model for the various characters my work often reenacts. The obsessive amateur who drifts from one discipline to another, adopting the signs of expertise but not expertise itself, is someone who can be found in many of my early works. Flaubert taught me the joy, power, and beauty of humor in critique. Each book on the list was a stepping-stone in finding my methodology and voice as an artist.

Many of your books look well-loved and thoroughly marked up. Are there certain books that you refer to often?

Indeed, each book I selected [for the top-ten list] is one that I return to often. It is more likely that I will reread these books than delve into new works.

Would you say that for you, making art requires a mix of influences and knowledge of many subjects? Do you learn from other disciplines?

I would not want to dictate what art making requires; however, the work that I do, and the art produced by artists who I most love and most learn from, certainly is in dialogue with a wide range of issues beyond art making. Many of the artists I know, while remaining extremely visual in their orientation, are keen researchers and voracious readers. They not only turn to books for knowledge but also actively engage institutions and collections, like the storerooms of natural history museums, print study centers, university special collections and archives, the overfilled homes of antiquarian collectors, meetings of political activists, and ecological field stations. The artists I know are peripatetic in the world of ideas, but I would also support the right of anyone to produce art in a bubble. My own interests often wander to the character of the amateur, who is activated by personal passion rather than the pursuit of fame, fortune, or glory. The contributions of amateurs to scientific and art endeavors are often significant, since they have insight from being self-trained outside of a discipline's doctrines. While I appreciate both fox and hedgehog, the fox tribe is undoubtedly my home.

**Top Ten Books
Mark Dion**

Herbert Spencer
Zim and Lester Ingle,
Seashores (A Golden
Nature Guide)

Lewis Carroll, *Alice
in Wonderland &
Through the Looking
Glass*

Dee Brown, *Bury
My Heart at
Wounded Knee*

William Beebe,
Jungle Days

Gustave Flaubert,
*Bouvard and
Pécuchet*

Henry Walter Bates,
*The Naturalist on
the River Amazons*

Oliver Impey and
Arthur MacGregor,
*The Origins of
Museums*

Alexander Wilson,
*The Culture of
Nature*

Celeste Olalquiaga,
*The Artificial
Kingdom*

Philipp Otto Runge,
Scherenschnitte

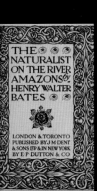

SEASHORES
475 MARINE SUBJECTS IN FULL COLOR
A GUIDE TO SHELLS, SEA PLANTS, SHORE BIRDS, AND OTHER NATURAL FEATURES OF AMERICAN COASTS
A GOLDEN NATURE GUIDE

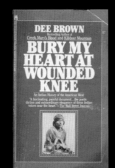

DEE BROWN
Bestselling Author of
Creek Mary's Blood and Killdeer Mountain
BURY MY HEART AT WOUNDED KNEE
An Indian History of the American West
"A fascinating, painful document...the poetic diction and extraordinary eloquence of these Indian voices near the heart."—The Wall Street Journal

JUNGLE DAYS
BY WILLIAM BEEBE

PENGUIN CLASSICS
GUSTAVE FLAUBERT
BOUVARD AND PÉCUCHET
WITH THE DICTIONARY OF RECEIVED IDEAS

THE NATURALIST ON THE RIVER AMAZONS by HENRY WALTER BATES
LONDON & TORONTO
PUBLISHED BY J M DENT & SONS LTD & IN NEW YORK BY E P DUTTON & CO

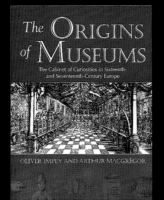

The ORIGINS of MUSEUMS
The Cabinet of Curiosities in Sixteenth- and Seventeenth-Century Europe
OLIVER IMPEY AND ARTHUR MACGREGOR

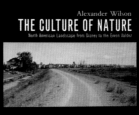

Alexander Wilson
THE CULTURE OF NATURE
North American Landscape from Disney to the Exxon Valdez

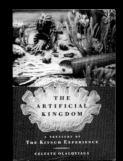

THE ARTIFICIAL KINGDOM
A TREASURY OF THE KITSCH EXPERIENCE
CELESTE OLALQUIAGA

PHILIPP OTTO RUNGE
SCHRIFTEN/SCHRIFTE

Tracey Emin

JO STEFFENS: There is a library in *The Great Gatsby* filled with books as intellectual "window dressing." How do you see book collections, or the role of a personal library, in this context?

TRACEY EMIN: I do sadly think a lot of people have intellectual window dressing. When I was younger I didn't like to show the books that I had read— it felt slightly show-offy and pretentious—but now I look at my books, the ones that I have read and really enjoyed, with a lot of sentimentality and with a lot of affection. My first edition of Alan Sillitoe's *The Loneliness of the Long-Distance Runner* is something I will treasure all my life. I am definitely one of those people that will carry a book around for months and months and months without reading it, but that's handbag dressing to make me feel good and never lonely.

Can you tell us about some of the ten books on your list that are especially important to you?

I read *Crime and Punishment* in 1984, at the same time as Billy Childish and my flatmate. [Emin and Childish met as students in 1981 and were boy-friend and girlfriend until 1985.] We had two copies between the three of us. It was unbearable if you were the one behind in the story—we would actually fight over the copies and go ballistic if any one of us gave the plot away. *My Cousin Rachel* is without a doubt one of the cruelest books I have ever read, and a great example of greed. I hated *The Black Swan*; once I had read the last page I threw it across the room in tears. I hated it because it was so sad, I hated the self-deception, I hated the fact that I could not decide what was right or what was wrong, the confusion of love and what is real. I related to this book very much. *An Education* is a short, shocking book that shows that even the smartest, brainiest girls can get fucked over by men who are out to con and take advantage. I love the self-effacing honesty. God how I wish I had read *Stargirl* when I was fifteen, it gave me so much hope. There's nothing wrong with being different, and it shows that it's actually a beautiful thing.

Are there works of fiction that helped you navigate through young adulthood? Were there heroes or heroines that you identified with?

Yes, definitely. *A Taste of Honey* by Shelagh Delaney, *Room at the Top* by John Braine, a number of the great British kitchen-sink writers, definitely helped me in my late teens and early twenties. I have the biggest disrespect and dislike for Emma in *Madame Bovary*; she's a fantastic role model for how a woman should never be, she infuriated me. Sylvia Plath—as much as she is a role model for a lot of young girls, I think suicide is a bad option and is over-romanticized in *The Bell Jar*.

Have you ever had to downsize your book collection?

When I was made homeless in 1987, my friends and I just got all our books and put them in super-market trollies and sold them for 5p each at the flea market. I kept a handful that I could carry, which I still have.

Are you a book collector? Do you look for that rare and beautiful book, or signed first edition?

I'm not someone who goes after first editions or beautifully bound copies. I just look for books with big print, as I'm finding it harder and harder to read small print, and these days it seems to be fashionable to print in tiny gray print! Faber & Faber and Black Sparrow used to make really beautiful paperback books.

Do you ever feel like you have too many books? Is there one book not in your library that you wish you owned?

Yes, I do, but there are worse things to own. I would like Céline's *Journey to the End of the Night* in really large print!

How are your books arranged? Do you have a system, do you stick to it, can you easily find the books you are looking for?

I have my Star Trek annuals under the subject of travel, which a journalist once said was very optimistic. But the majority of my books are just not in any real order, which infuriates me—one day they will be. My work library, with all the books that feature me, is in such strict order—by date, subject, alphabetically, beyond OCD—yet my personal collection is just really eclectic and all over the place. Every time I am looking for a book to read, it's like going into a secondhand bookshop—I never know what I'm going to come across. I am also at the age now where I have forgotten books that I have read, so it's like rediscovering them all over again.

What is the role of literature in your life? Is it as important as art history, and what does it mean for your art practice?

In a bizarre way, I shouldn't say this, but it's more important. When I read a really good book, my mind is filled with a million images, and for me it's like having a friend. Having a good book means I never feel lonely. Art can do this, but it is momentary; literature fills me, it makes me feel cozy.

Do you believe books can have a kind of special power over us, and if so, what is it about books that have this effect?

Yes, some books do. Some books are just pages of writing, and other have this magic that has transformative power. You know there are some books that after you read them, you are never the same person, but it's different books for different people.

At what age did you begin to seek out books? Did you use the library when you were young?

I used to go to the library, but it was more for somewhere to play when it was cold. Margate's new library was amazing, but I didn't read a book on my own until I was seventeen. I was ill, and my mum bought me a book on Greta Garbo. And then there was no stopping me; I went from reading Hollywood biographies to Russian classics within a matter of weeks. David Niven's *The Moon's a Balloon* has a lot to answer for.

Top Ten Books
Tracey Emin

Fyodor Dostoyevsky,
*Crime and
Punishment*

Gustave Flaubert,
Madame Bovary

Daphne du Maurier,
My Cousin Rachel

Vladimir Nabokov,
Laughter in the Dark

F. Scott Fitzgerald,
The Great Gatsby

Jerry Spinelli, *Stargirl*

Lynn Barber,
An Education

Thomas Mann,
The Black Swan

Gary Indiana, *I Can
Give You Anything
But Love*

Benedict de
Spinoza, *Ethics*

SIGNET CLASSIC

CRIME AND PUNISHMENT

FYODOR DOSTOYEVSKY

A BRILLIANT TRANSLATION BY THE NOTED
SCHOLAR AND CRITIC, SIDNEY MONAS
UNABRIDGED

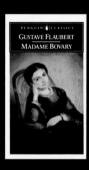

PENGUIN CLASSICS

Gustave Flaubert

Madame Bovary

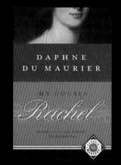

DAPHNE DU MAURIER

My Cousin
Rachel

VLADIMIR NABOKOV

laughter
in the
dark

The GREAT
GATSBY

F·SCOTT·FITZGERALD

JERRY SPINELLI

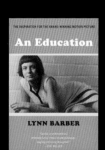

THE INSPIRATION FOR THE AWARD-WINNING MOTION PICTURE

An Education

LYNN BARBER

Thomas Mann

THE
BLACK
SWAN

With an Introduction by
Nina Pelikan Straus

. . .

The Ethics of
SPINOZA

The Road To Inner Freedom Baruch Spinoza

Rome

Phaidon – When Pictures Vanish

SIGMAR POLKE · MOCA · Schimmel

JUERGEN TELLER · Do You Know What I Mean

JUERGEN TELLER · Vivienne Westwood Spring Summer 2003

The Couture Accessory

All Hawaii Entitées / Lunar Reggae · Irish Museum of Modern Art

iWITNESS tomStoddart

CATHERINE GRENIER · annette messager · Flammarion

AGENT ORANGE · 'COLLATERAL DAMAGE' IN VIET NAM · A Tribute to Werner Bischof · PHILIP JONES GRIFFITHS

Brigid Keenan · Damascus Hidden Treasures of the Old City

NEUE CUISINE THE ELEGANT TASTES OF VIENNA

Our World in Focus

Australia Exposed · Jason Kimberley · Moving Towards a Sustainable Future · earth pledge

FOR EVER GODARD!

THE SEX BOOK SUZI GODSON

marilyn monroe · fragments

Visual charades. What has an ox to do with the letter A? The art of looking sideways. How to turn knots into bows. When does 1 and 1 add up to 3? Why sit with your back to the view? Notes on the · Alan Fletcher · Φ

BRIGHT!
BRIGHT!
TYPOGRAPHY BETWEEN ILLUSTRATION AND ART
TYPOGRAPHY BETWEEN ILLUSTRATION AND ART

Céline Delavaux
KUNST, DIE SIE NIE SEHEN WERDEN
GESTOHLEN VERSCHOLLEN ZERSTÖRT
PRESTEL

DANGER! Women Artists at Work
MERRELL

DANGER! Women Artists at Work
MERRELL

Joanna Norman
HANDMADE IN BRITAIN
V&A

Joanna Norman
HANDMADE IN BRITAIN
V&A

THE COLONY ROOM CLUB, 1948–2008
A HISTORY OF BOHEMIAN SOHO BY SOPHIE PARKIN

DESERT ISLAND DISCS
70 YEARS OF CASTAWAYS
BANTAM PRESS

Creative Thinking
CJ Hollins

WITH THE HAND

WITH THE HAND

Affektpolitik und Raum
Heidi Helmhold
34

WHY YOUR FIVE YEAR OLD COULD NOT HAVE DONE THAT
Susie Hodge

TWENTYEIGHT FINGERS

L'ALTRO RITRATTO
MJR
Ɛr
PRESTEL

L'ALTRO RITRATTO
MJR
Ɛr
PRESTEL

Women Artists of the New Millennium
THE RECKONING
PRESTEL

Women Artists of the New Millennium
THE RECKONING
PRESTEL

4⁹ for English
4⁹ for English

text in textile art
BATSFORD

Obrist

Obrist

Obrist

Time Warns

STEVE JONES

ALMOST LIKE A WHALE

IMAGES OF SHOW BUSINESS — EDITED BY JAMES FOWLER

A CENTURY OF WAR — AND THE NEW WORLD ORDER — WILLIAM ENGDAHL

AN ILLUSTRATED ENCYCLOPEDIA OF TRADITIONAL SYMBOLS

Sacred Geometry

THE STAR TREK ENCYCLOPEDIA — A Reference Guide to the Future — UPDATED AND EXPANDED EDITION — MICHAEL OKUDA AND DENISE OKUDA

NIGHTMARES OF NATURE — Richard Matthews

Played in Manchester — Simon Inglis

THE ROLLING STONES — Robert Palmer

SS REGALIA — Maurizio Terzini

ROBIN LUMSDEN — Something Italian — PENGUIN LANTERN

Intersection

into the

Watson and Mark Hix...

BSM Driving — Theory Test — Pass Your Driving — Revised 1998

THE ENCYCLOPEDIA OF NORTH AMERICAN INDIAN TRIBES — BILL YENNE — CRESCENT BOOKS

BSM Pass Your Driving Test

BIXTREE — SOUTH PARK A STICKYFORMS ADVENTURE! — MELCHER MEDIA

MARTIN LEMAN'S COMIC & CURIOUS CATS — DAVID TAYLOR — GOLLANCZ

KLIMT

HOFFMANN

PIONEERS OF
MODERNISM

▲ PRESTEL

Egon Schiele
Self-Portraits and Portraits

Agnes Husslein-Arco and Jane Kallir

belvedere

▲ PRESTEL

THE LIFE AND TIMES OF DANTE

Country Life

PAUL HAMLYN

ROYAL FAMILY

GODFREY TALBOT

EGON SCHIELE. WOMEN.

RICHARD NAGY LTD

Abstract Expressionism

MoMA

The World Upside Down

Turner Contemporary | Loam Books

MARGATE'S SEASIDE HERITAGE

THE ROYAL PARKS

Vivienne Westwood

Gene Krell

fashion memoir

VERSO

Bento's Sketchbook

JOHN BERGER

Best in Show

Sally Muir &
Joanna Osborne

C&B

COX COOKIES & CAKE

Eric Lanlard & Patrick Cox

MITCHELL
BEAZLEY

TRAVEL SECRETS
TANYA ROSE

The rule of luxury travel

MR
MASON ROSE
PUBLISHING

Nothing in the World But Youth

Turner Contemporary

richard
prince

american
prayer

bibliothèque
nationale
de france

gagosian
gallery

collection agnès b.

JR

TRAVEL SECRETS
TANYA ROSE

The rule of luxury travel

MR
MASON ROSE
PUBLISHING

LANCELOT OF THE LAKE

TRACY
CHEVALIER

Remarkable Creatures

HARPER

The Promise of Photography

Luminita Sabau Ed.

Prestel

THE 20TH CENTURY ART BOOK

GERMAN PAINTING

MARLBOROUGH 2006

A SUMMER EXHIBITION

MARLBOROUGH LONDON 2007

GARRARD

MÚLTIPLAS DIMENSÕES

A CENTURY OF OLYMPIC POSTERS

MARGARET TIMMERS

V&A

UNDERCOVER SURREALISM Ades and Baker

Eva Hesse Drawing

Catherine de Zegher

The Drawing Center

atelier one

THE EMBASSY
THE EMBASSY

Dark Matter

ROYAL ACADEMY ILLUSTRATED 2006

WHITE CUBE

RA

JAARVERSLAG / ANNUAL REPORT 2005

Stedelijk Museum

THE STONEMASON
BY 'CHYLDISH'

L-13

II BEYOND NOSE TO TAIL

FERGUS HENDERSON &
JUSTIN PIERS GELLATLY

Bloomberg SPACE contemporaries 2006

Theaster
Gates

JO STEFFENS: Can you tell us how you became interested in libraries and books?

THEASTER GATES: I've had an interest in books for a long time, but sometimes these things are born out of a deficit. While there were books all around me, I always loved them as objects. I loved old things, and I think books were in my reach; it was within my capacity to acquire a book at a time. And I developed an early love for art books and artist books.

Do you collect artist books?

I would not call myself a collector of anything, although I have a lot of things, but I do have a collection of artist books. When I was in college I started to bind books, and my knowledge of binding is a big part of my knowledge of craft. I've also made my own artist books, and I have a small collection of those. Early on I made bound versions of my poetry, and forms of scrapping or collage, for pieces that were too small for a work of art. I was using natural linen, hemp, and heavier paper stock, and in Seattle I learned Armenian Coptic binding; it was a good way to be precise. Before I knew it, I had probably bound a couple hundred journals. This is a part of my life I have not talked about much—looking closely at spines and how they were done, and figuring out how special-edition books were made. All of the architecture of a book is very interesting to me, and there really is an important kind of micro-architecture in the book that I think is worth thinking about. I spend a lot of time just looking at them.

Did you apprentice with a bookmaker?

No, I just took some classes and figured it out. The Armenian Coptic binding class was the hardest class I ever took. It gave me an idea of how books are crafted, and then I just started to play with it. I use a very simple book, with a stapled binding, to keep all my notes in. It's a little folded thing that I make myself, and staple together out of scrap paper and construction paper, and it really holds up.

Are you attracted to books because they are easy to acquire and make?

As an artist, I think about how content is presented and about how the page is like its own little world where there are a lot of decisions you can make about how the content is presented, like whether there are drawings or writings. When I was writing a lot of poetry, I was super interested in the spatial layout of words, and the way language played out on a page. It allows you this micro-world that is super affordable, and allows you all this freedom. When maybe the rest of the world is too big to actually have an impact, you can always go to the page.

How did Dorchester Projects get its start? Did you approach Prairie Avenue Art and Architecture Bookstore? [Dorchester Projects houses a small library including 14,000 volumes from the now-closed Prairie Avenue Art and Architecture Bookstore.]

It kind of caught me off guard, because when I went to the store Bill Hasbrouck was there with his assistants, and people were really sad. They were buying their one or two books as keepsakes, and I just went up to Bill and said, "These books should really stay together." I didn't really think I had the capacity to buy them all; I was just making a statement. When he did offer them to me, it meant all of a sudden that it was less about the books and more about the logistics; how was I going to move five hundred boxes, how do I do this in a week? The blessing was also the curse, in that it was a real effort. Then over time I came to embrace the effort of saving collections, and I created an infrastructure that could manage the faithful transition of a collection of things from the original owner to another owner, and I have really come to take a lot of pleasure in that, and making up spaces along the way that could be the exact poetic response to the availability of a new inventory in the world.

Do you consider the Dorchester Projects Library and Archive to be a kind of house museum?

With the archive house and the listening house I am always asking, How does one make a special place? And what are the designations of special places, so that other people feel they have the right, and the permission, to come to them? A house museum sounds like a place you should visit. In some ways, yes, the archive house is a house museum, but it is dormant in a way, and not always active, so it is really waiting for the right moment to fully bloom. For that to happen, it needs the right set of circumstances—kind of like the Stony Island Arts Bank, which is a big house museum. I am excited for these smaller spaces in my neighborhood to wake up, for volunteers and staff to fly open the doors so that great things can happen.

Considering you have amassed a vast library and archive, what is your relationship to the physical, or analog, as opposed to the digital world?

I try to live in an analog world as much as I can. With the slides [approximately 60,000 glass lantern slides from the University of Chicago's Art History Department], and books, there is the pleasure of touch for me; the ability to reach in and pull a thing out of its carton, to smell it. All of that other sensorial activity is very important to me and actually helps me read better, see better, memorize better, and understand an object better. Because I am such a visual person and I enjoy material so much, I think that I pay more attention to whatever is on a beautiful object. In some ways, the way I learned art history was because it was presented to me on glass slides and not on a computer. The digital era is going to make the material world even more fetishistic. Soon you will have fewer and fewer places where you can touch old things, or you will have to be an expert to have access to old things.

What role can the private or independent library play in the community?

My hope is that, especially around the library, we help young people recognize how amazingly intimate, and attractive, and seductive reading can be as a pleasure, and we would really not apologize for that. Libraries are not just about the books on the shelves—they are also about the community they create, and so using these places and spaces to convene community is really important. What I found is that books are often the perfect backdrop for getting new conversations started, and a way of breaking crazy silences, and in my case a way to increase knowledge. There is probably no way that I will read every book that I now have in my collection, but it gives me just endless pleasure attempting to.

Do you think this appetite for books, or reading, is present in the current generation of students?

We are definitely much more of an image-based culture now. It seems like there are still some areas where reading is an important part of life, but then most people would rather just read the Cliffs Notes. I think it is unfortunate because we are a world that has always known and understood literature and writing, and I hope that continues, even though we are switching from the book to a PDF, that we would always make room for looking for the nuances within language. Part of the reason I feel so connected to collecting is because it becomes kind of an index to understanding the world, and people.

Would you say making art requires a mix of influences? Do you learn from other disciplines?

I think part of the complexity of my artistic practice is that I refuse to just read about art; I am constantly looking at other things, and those things have a substantial influence on me.

How do you decide what to read? Do you visit your own library?

Yes. Sometimes I will see a title, or an author, or an artist, and I'll think, Oh wow, like with Edward Kienholz, an artist who is important to my work, or I could be looking at a Bruce Nauman book and come across the diary of Anne Frank. There are these little moments when you say to yourself, "I would love to read the first chapter of Anne Frank." Those encounters can happen very easily when you allow them to happen.

Carrie Mae Weems said she wanted you as one of her favorite books.

That's awesome, but I cannot be bound!

Is there one book that stands out as having had a big impact on you when you first read it?

Henri Lefebvre's book *The Production of Space*. I read it as an undergrad in 1992. It was the first time that I understood that the world's land, or space, could be read not only as an emotional and spiritual place but also as economic and political. And that there was a world of imagination about space that could then make space a concrete place. That, in a way, we have the capacity to imagine space, and to transform it, and that some of those transformations can be productive toward a social good, and sometimes they can be productive toward a capital good. It forever shifted the way I saw myself in the world as related to a place, and a space.

Top Ten Books
Theater Gates

Gloria Moure,
Gordon Matta-Clark: Works and Collected Writings

Jacques Villon,
Raymond Duchamp-Villon, and Marcel Duchamp, *The Brothers Duchamp*

Bernard Leach,
Hamada, Potter

William S. Rubin,
Dada and Surrealist Art

Tom McDonough,
ed., *Guy Debord and the Situationist International: Texts and Documents*

Mary Louise Clifford,
From Slavery to Freetown: Black Loyalists after the American Revolution

John L. Thomas, ed.,
Slavery Attacked: The Abolitionist Crusade

Arts and Crafts Essays by Members of the Arts and Crafts Exhibition

Gordon Matta-Clark
Works and Collected Writings
Gloria Moure

Ediciones Polígrafa

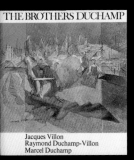

THE BROTHERS DUCHAMP

Jacques Villon
Raymond Duchamp-Villon
Marcel Duchamp

HAMADA

potter

Bernard Leach

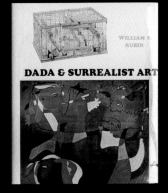

WILLIAM S. RUBIN

DADA & SURREALIST ART

ARAKI

LOVE AND DEATH

HISTORY OF THE FAN

G. WOOLLISCROFT RHEAD

Guy Debord
AND THE
SITUATIONIST
INTERNATIONAL

TEXTS AND DOCUMENTS

edited by Tom McDonough

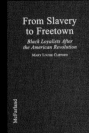

From Slavery
to Freetown

*Black Loyalists After
the American Revolution*

MARY LOUISE CLIFFORD

McFarland

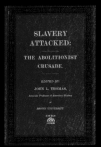

SLAVERY
ATTACKED:

THE ABOLITIONIST
CRUSADE.

EDITED BY

JOHN L. THOMAS,
Associate Professor of American History
AT
BROWN UNIVERSITY

ARTS AND CRAFTS ESSAYS
BY MEMBERS OF THE ARTS
AND CRAFTS EXHIBITION
SOCIETY

SPLENDOR · Late Roman Painting · DUROI · ARCHAIC GREEK YOUTHS · PHAIDON · HERB ALPERT ELAM · THE EARTH, THE TEMPLE AND THE GODS · YALE · THE MUSIC AND MUSICAL INSTRUMENTS OF JAPAN · PIGGOTT · 1893 · THE POPE ASSASSINATED · RAPHAEL · PREHISTORIC POTTERY IN EGYPT · OLAFUR ELIASSON · PROJECT RAINBOW · TUTMANS · SEAN SCULLY · the Essential Cy Twombly · Christian Marclay · AUF DEM DACH · ON THE ROOF · DAS AKTFOTO · FREUD

OFFICE GRAY CASE · BRANDON LATTU · TAMAYO · Richard Paul Lohse · Konstruktive Gebrauchsgrafik · MOSAÏQUE TRÉSOR DE LA LATINITÉ · ars latina · Picasso POSTERS · LUIS CARLOS RODRIGO · ★★★★ · ARTE EDICIONES · Picasso POSTERS · LUIS CARLOS RODRIGO · ★★ · ARTE EDICIONES · Picasso POSTERS · LUIS CARLOS RODRIGO · ★ · ARTE EDICIONES · Picasso POSTERS · LUIS CARLOS RODRIGO · ★★★ · ARTE EDICIONES · MASTERPIECES OF INDIAN SCULPTURE From The NASLI M. HEERAMANECK Collections · MASTERPIECES OF PRIMITIVE ART · MASTERPIECES OF IVORY FROM THE WALTERS ART GALLERY · MORROW · JAMES ENSOR 1873-1902 XAVIER TRICOT · JAMES ENSOR 1907-1941 XAVIER TRICOT · GREAT HOUSES OF ITALY: THE TUSCAN VILLAS · NANCY OUTSIDE IN JULY · VIKING · BRONZES SCULPTORS FOUNDERS · Berman · Abage · CANADIAN TEXTILE · LADANYI · COLLEGES · MATIGNON GALLERY · Kai Althoff · Gebärden und Ausdruck · NEW VISION Photographs of the American West · PICASSO CUBISM 1907 - 1917

Wangechi
Mutu

WANGECHI MUTU: It's very artsy. My library is actually organized by color at this point. And part of the reason for that is that I have a visual memory. So I know where my *Flash of the Spirit* is because it has a red spine. When I was a kid, it was a sad moment when I moved from the books with pictures to books with no pictures at all—not even photographs. The books in my more serious library are organized by color to make them accessible through the visual of the spine.

Then I have another library that I consider my research and archive library, with books from exhibitions or from artists that I really respect and am inspired by. And there are two categories: books that I know I need all the time, and books that I always come back to, for instance Francesco Clemente, or Egon Schiele, or Chris Ofili's drawings. There are some that I need an eight-foot ladder for, and some that I need a five-foot ladder for.

Do you consider your library a collection? Are you a collecting person?

I am the ultimate collecting person, but I am not so fetishistic about it. Meaning, I don't necessarily get first editions, and I should, but I don't. I collect things for my work, and I treat books the same way. The actual physical book is important to me. And it probably dates me a little bit; it's a bit old-school. I like to know something through the tactile, the information that it has to give me.

Do you annotate your books habitually?

I used to. As a student I used to annotate tremendously in books, for various reasons, for class work and for myself. Now I do drawings and I leave them inside. I always leave things in the book that remind me of that moment.

I couldn't help but notice that you actually have a bookshelf on your website. Do you consider this to be a virtual bookshelf?

What I wanted from my website is the experience of the artist's thinking process. I have a deep love of studios and the way studios function for artists. So I wanted to make sure that people know that, as well as about the art that I make, I am also very thrilled and excited about the writing that has been done about my work and things that relate to my work that other artists are involved in. But I love to look at libraries—and I go to people's homes for dinner, or for whatever—I am the consummate voyeur, I like to snoop… I open up medical cabinets and I look at libraries, these are my two favorite things.

Do you consider your own books as artworks in themselves?

The first book I did, *The Shady Promise*, was kind of a labor of love. It was about my intense desire to talk about my work in terms of a progressive learning process, starting from drawing all the way to installation. I came out of a sculpture background, but I got into painting and drawing, which is how people got to know me. Some people can create work really beautifully on the move, but I was doing video, and I was doing installation, and I only had this tiny studio. So I started drawing. So *Shady Promise* is very much about digging into the layers of my past and how I evolved as an artist. I was very lucky early in my career. This wonderful woman, Lauri Firstenberg, was getting rid of a lot of her African art books. So I have used a lot of those books physically in my work. And that to me is almost sacrilegious, to cut a book up to use it for material, but though I consider it material, it's almost sacred. It's not the image only, it's also the fact that it came out of a book that was talking about a specific kind of history of art. I love that. And then I combine that with more frivolous and highly recirculated magazine imagery and try to see if the two can have a conversation.

When you cut up those books and made the imagery part of the collage, was this source material knowledge that only you had, or did it become a readable and integrated part of your work?

In some cases people get it, they know it. Because I am not changing the scale, I am not changing the color, so if you have looked at a certain book and you have looked at a certain magazine you notice that's that garment, or these are the beads from that particular ethnicity in West Africa, whatever it is. So it is traceable, but I think it all depends on what people have been looking at. But I don't make it overtly legible; it's not didactic in that way. It's a lot more like a soup. It's more churned in there, and it affects the way the overall image looks.

In your book *This You Call Civilization?* you included excerpts from books that frame the issues of colonialism that your work addresses. Was that didactic impulse also part of the exhibition?

No. That was the idea of the curator. He had been to a few of my lectures, and I had shown images of Zora Neale Hurston and talked about how she mined the Africanisms of English America. There is also [Adam Hochschild's] *King Leopold's Ghost* in there—it's amazing that that was produced when it was—and [Caroline Elkins's] *Britain's Gulag*, about the Kenyan Mau Mau; it's important to see these things together.

Which brings me to your ten books, as they are kind of in the same orbit as the books you were just talking about. Do you look for a shared experience within this triangulation between the Americas, Europe, and Africa? Do you consider your own books, or books in general, to be an asset for activism?

I think they can be. I think *The Grapes of Wrath* is one of those books. It's about the Great Depression and about the time the Americans were moving to the West. It's about a time when everyone was poor. It wasn't a time when one particular color or type of person was poor. There was this phenomenal photographer of the Depression, Dorothea Lange, and this incredible image of a [migrant] mother that she took was reproduced in the copy of *Grapes of Wrath* that I read. That book impacted me so much, as someone coming from a poor country, because Steinbeck wrote about the struggle of

life for people across the country for the most basic things. It wasn't the America that I was about to move into, it's an America that has grown out of that, and that has forgotten what that time was.

There is a constellation that my books create, that is a marker, a drawing of how I think. But they all come out of specific times in my life, like Patricia Williams's *Alchemy of Race and Rights*. I don't even know why I picked up that book, but it's almost one of those serendipitous spiritual things. Williams talks about pedagogy and race and gender, and she is brilliant because she is a lawyer, but she is also writing the book for kids, for young people, for older people, and so I read that book and I kept going back to it because I was realizing my growth, my consciousness; my blackness was being described, as well.

And then *Flash of the Spirit*—the copy I have of this book now is definitely not the copy I had when I first read it, because that book was a mess by the time I was done with it. It was in my bag all the time when I really was looking at the synchronicity of cultures, oppressed or colonized culture, or the mixing of cultures, and how a culture can still exist within this place of being oppressed. I was looking for my African self in America. *Things Fall Apart* was also another one of these books, as was *The God of Small Things*.

Are there other epiphanies from your top-ten list that we have not yet talked about?

Americanah was great. I was having a moment where I could not articulate clearly some of the immigrant experiences that I was going through, because I happened to be a funny kind of undocumented immigrant just a few years ago. I was one of these people where you would think, You can't possibly be undocumented—as to say, illegal—because you have an Ivy League education, and you came with a student ID, how is it possible? And it was also a moment where I felt like I couldn't feel authentically about Africa and Kenya, because I hadn't been back for so long.

**Top Ten Books
Wangechi Mutu**

Chimamanda Ngozi
Adichie, *Americanah*

Robert Farris
Thompson, *Flash
of the Spirit: African
and Afro-American
Art and Philosophy*

Patricia J. Williams,
*The Alchemy of Race
and Rights: Diary
of a Law Professo*r

Chinua Achebe,
Things Fall Apart

James Baldwin,
Another Country

Claudia Rankine,
*Citizen: An
American Lyric*

Arundhati Roy,
*The God of
Small Things*

John Steinbeck,
The Grapes of Wrath

Toni Morrison,
God Help the Child

K. Sello Duiker,
*The Quiet Violence
of Dreams*

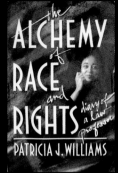

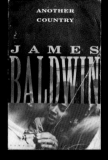

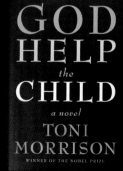

THE IN-BETWEEN WORLD OF VIKRAM LALL · M. G. Vassanji

BLACK LOOKS · The Complete Works of LAO TZU & HUA HU CHING · bell hooks · Tao Te Ching · HUA-CHING NI

ELECTRIC GYPSY · HARRY SHAPIRO & CAESAR GLEBBEEK · ST. MARTIN'S PRESS

NEXT · edited by ERIC LIU · NORTON

James Ngugi · A Grain of Wheat · HEB · 36

THE TESTAMENT OF MARY · THE AWAKENING and SELECTED STORIES · COLM TÓIBÍN

V.S. NAIPAUL · THE ENIGMA OF ARRIVAL

ONE HUNDRED YEARS OF SOLITUDE · GABRIEL GARCÍA MÁRQUEZ · AVON

New Black Playwrights · William Couch, Jr.

Anne Carson · GLASS, IRONY AND GOD · NDP808

Mandela's Way · Richard Stengel · CROWN

THE SOUND AND THE FURY · SECOND EDITION · NORTON CRITICAL EDITIONS

FAULKNER

THE BEAUTY MYTH · NAOMI WOLF · ANCHOR BOOKS

GOULD · THE FLAMINGO'S SMILE · NORTON

WESCHLER · SEEING IS FORGETTING THE NAME OF THE THING ONE SEES · CALIFORNIA

SRI ISOPANISAD · His Divine Grace A.C. Bhaktivedanta Swami Prabhupāda

Barbara Gowdy · THE WHITE BONE · PICADOR · U S A

HEAD · MARU · HEINEMANN · a w s

THE SECOND SEX · Simone de Beauvoir · VINTAGE

DESTINED TO WITNESS · GROWING UP BLACK IN NAZI GERMANY · Hans J. Massaquoi · Perennial

Peoples and Cultures of Kenya — Fedders • Salvadori — Transafrica • KIDC

The Last Gift — ABDULRAZAK GURNAH

HURSTON — I Love Myself — When I Am Laughing.... And Then Again When I Am Looking Mean and Impressive — THE FEMINIST PRESS

HUXLEY — THE FLAME TREES OF THIKA

LEAKEY — WHITE AFRICAN — Schenkman

IN OTHER WORLDS — GAYATRI CHAKRAVORTY SPIVAK — Routledge

flyboy in the buttermilk — greg tate — contemporary america — PANTHEON

MAUS — II — SPIEGELMAN — PANTHEON

THE MOUNTAIN PEOPLE — Turnbull — Touchstone — SIMON & SCHUSTER

Shaw — Colonial Inscriptions

Weed — Wise Woman Herbal — HEALING WISE

DEREK WALCOTT — COLLECTED POEMS 1948–1984 — FSG

The House on Mango Street — Sandra Cisneros — Wake up and open your eyes — EDWARD MUNHRE — VINTAGE

VOICE OF AMERICA — E. C. OSONDU

Fiction — Colin Channer — waiting in vain — ONE WORLD Ballantine Books

CHAMOISEAU — Creole Folktales

Appiah — IN MY FATHER'S HOUSE — The New Press

BLACK AFRICAN CINEMA

TRINH — FRAMER FRAMED — Routledge

One Hundred Years of Solitude — GABRIEL GARCÍA MÁRQUEZ

RICHARDS

INSIDE THE STUDIO

TWO DECADES OF TALKS WITH ARTISTS IN NEW YORK

INDEPENDENT CURATORS INTERNATIONAL

ICI

MY NAME IS ASHER LEV

a novel

Anchor Books

CHAIM POTOK

Three Famous Short Novels
William Faulkner

Vintage

CANDIDE · VOLTAIRE

SPOSO manuale d'istruzioni

Shandon Fowler

THE MALAISE OF MODERNITY

Anansi

KO#; ALEKI

TAYLOR

Kevin Young

TO REPEL GHOSTS

LEAVES OF GRASS

· · WHITMAN

Illustrated by
CHARLES CULLEN

Z
ZOLAND BOOKS

BERLIN BIENNALE

平

FORGET FEAR

KW

We Won't Budge

An African Exile in the World

MANTHIA DIAWARA

Helinand Peed e g&gag&ag

AIRING DIRTY LAUNDRY

Addison Wesley

A-184

Sphereland Burger

THE UNABRIDGED JOURNALS OF SYLVIA PLATH

EDITED BY KAREN V. KUKIL

ANCHOR BOOKS

Ed Davis

Paraph of Bone &
Other Kinds of Blue

AFR

kwani?

LO

QUILL

Coming of Age in Samoa

Margaret Mead

Ann Hamilton

São Paulo · Seattle

Henry Art Gallery

Martin Parr

JO STEFFENS: You have one of the most important collections of photography books ever assembled. When did you start to dedicate yourself to this pursuit?

MARTIN PARR: I just started collecting books at college, and as I became wealthier, I was able to accelerate the collecting. Have you seen the series I've done on photobooks? [*The Photobook: A History*, three volumes.] It is an obsession, and you carry on and you keep going. Because I was collecting books from territories that no one really had collected from, it became quite exciting to have the chase—there's always a territory I am chasing. I am currently buying books from the early days of Solidarity. I have a source in Poland who is able to buy at auction, and it's amazing, absolutely unbelievable; I didn't know these existed. I also just purchased a protest book from Thailand from 1973. To my knowledge no one has this material at all; that's what is exciting, you are finding things that no one even knew existed, let alone has. Some of these are really badly printed, but that's part of their charm really.

Can you describe your library and how it's organized? Do you have themes, sections, and subcategories— can you easily find the books you are looking for?

It's organized pretty haphazardly. I have a big building where all the modern and contemporary books are kept, and in my house I keep a lot of the other stuff; sometimes they're grouped by territory, sometimes they are just on the shelf. My Chinese books are in the other building, and the Japanese and Latin American books are downstairs. There are themes that I collect, and I do have a special shelf with protest books. It's an interesting topic; I have a few books about the American student protest movement and riots in the 1960s.

You have tens of thousands of books in your collection; how did you go about selecting the ten titles for our list—and can you tell us something about them?

I wrote down the first ten books that came into my head straight away. I believe the *Complete Photo*

Story of Till Murder Case is regarded as the first civil rights book. It was self-published in 1955 by Ernest Withers, and it cost $1.00 originally. It took me twenty years to find a copy, and I paid £7,000 for it. Another book, *What Makes Men Tick,* must have arrived the week you asked me for the list— it would be different if you asked me now. I have a whole section of books that are sort of weird, and they usually come from America.

Henri Cartier-Bresson dedicated a copy of *The Decisive Moment* to you, and he personally "corrected" the title to say "The (more or less) Decisive Moment(s)." What can you tell us about that?

We famously had a spat, Cartier-Bresson and myself, so that's why it's interesting to have the dedication in there, where he said I was from another planet. That's what makes that quite significant, having the signature from him to me. He always changed the slight "typo" in the title; he did that consistently, not just in my book.

Has the role of the printed book, as an historical artifact, changed now that it's possible to publish digitally on many different platforms?

It's changed, but I just acquired the five books from the Umbrella protest in Hong Kong, so even though the main dissemination of its images was on the Internet, there were still five printed books produced. They may have been distributed in smaller quantities, from five hundred to two thousand copies each; I don't know much about the history of them.

In late 2015 five Hong Kong–based booksellers went missing and eventually turned up in the custody of mainland Chinese authorities. Did you follow that story?

All the people who have been abducted are people who were selling frothy books on Xi Jinping and such [published by Mighty Current]. They are not photography books, but if you are a collector you should probably get them.

How does the photobook compare to the written word in its capacity to document cultural history?

You are speaking to the converted here.

Do you believe that artists and photographers can live beyond their time through their books?

I think a book is a great legacy for any photographer because it does live on, and people don't tend to throw them away.

Do you use books in the exhibits that you curate?

I sent fifty books to the Barbican for a show I had, *Strange and Familiar*, about photographers who came from abroad to photograph in the UK. The books bring the show alive, and you cannot imagine now a show like that without the books in it. Twenty years ago that would have been impossible.

Is there one book that stands out as having had a big influence on you when you first read it?

I liked *The Americans* and Tony Ray-Jones's *A Day Off*. The Robert Frank was the first book I bought. *The Americans* is a classic; it is one of the greatest photo essays ever produced. Tony Ray-Jones is a British photographer who died very young, and *A Day Off* was published a couple of years after he died. It was great to see that book finally come out, and to see the work printed. There have been many Tony Ray-Jones books published since then, but it was the first in 1974.

Is there a question that you do not get asked about your library, but wish to be asked?

Not very many people interview me about my library; in fact, this might be my first library-only interview. I usually get interviewed about other things because I'm very active on other fronts, like curating, editing, and being a photographer.

Carrie Mae Weems has The Sweet Flypaper of Life on her list of top books, and you own a copy as well. What makes this book significant?

I have a copy that was inscribed and signed by Langston Hughes in 1955, and autographed by the photographer, Roy DeCarava, in 1984.

Are you influenced by other disciplines? Do you read novels?

Not really. I watch films, but they do not particularly influence my photography. I've accumulated enough to have a good knowledge of photography and so I understand the language, and I'm aware of that as I go forward. I don't particularly relish novels; I don't read them in fact. My studio has an Instagram account, so I'll see what that is doing, but I don't get involved in it. I have faith in other people doing it for me.

Do you have anything else you would like to say about your library?

I spend all of my time now lending books to people. I always lend them to public institutions. It's a big job now just dealing with all of the loans, especially as I am not home much. Eventually my book collection will probably end up in the Tate, or somewhere like that.

**Top Ten Books
Martin Parr**

Chris Killip,
In Flagrante

Ernest Withers,
*Complete Photo
Story of Till
Murder Case*

Daido Moriyama,
*Shashin yo
Sayonara / Bye, Bye
Photography, Dear*

Nicolas Simarik,
La Déroute

Portia Beers, *What
Makes Men Tick*
(Woman Alive!
series)

Luc Chessex, *The
Face of the Revolu-
tion: Photographic
Essay on the Images
of Fidel Castro in
Cuba*

Evgeny Vasin,
Just Life

Hans Bellmer, *Les
Jeux de la poupée*,
with poems
by Paul Éluard

Gian Butturini,
London

Cornell Capa,
*The Concerned
Photographer*

COMPLETE PHOTO STORY OF TILL MURDER CASE

FIRST AND ONLY
COMPLETE, FACTUAL
PHOTO STORY
OF TILL CASE

AUTHENTIC PICTURES
TAKEN ON THE SPOT
DESIGNED TO MEET
PUBLIC DEMAND

price: $1.00

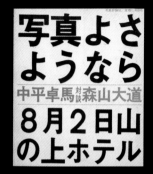

写真よさ
ようなら
中平卓馬 対談 森山大道
8月2日山
の上ホテル

LA DÉROUTE

WOMAN ALIVE

What Makes
Men Tick

просто
ЖИЗНЬ
ФОТОГРАФИИ

HANS BELLMER
LES JEUX DE LA POUPÉE
ILLUSTRÉS DE TEXTES PAR PAUL ÉLUARD

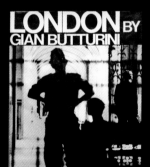

LONDON BY
GIAN BUTTURINI

the concerned
photographer

俗神 ★ ZOKUSHIN　H. TSUCHIDA　IHED

天竺 渡辺眸　野幻舎

いま　MIKIYA TAKIMOTO SIGHTS EING　LITTLE MORE　大橋仁　青幻舎

写真との対話　修羅の圏　森山大道

写真 都市 TOKYO　JAPAN NEW MAP　BLACK SUN, THE EYES OF FOUR.　東京都市写真館

冷蔵庫　ICE BOX　Aspects of Contemporary Photography　現代写真の動向　潮田登久子　Shinichiro Kobayashi　APERTURE　Bed Books　KAWASAKI CITY MUSEUM

東松照明作品集　発　森山大道　Haru Museum　日本の写真家37　PARCO出版

職 WORK 1990-1995　視線 The Look　橋口譲二 Hashiguchi George　橋口譲二 Hashiguchi George　SUGIMOTO PORTRAITS　Guggenheim museum

十七歳の地図　Seventeen's Map　橋口譲二 HASHIGUCHI George　文藝春秋　文藝春秋

OBSESSION　HIROSHI YODA

鉄火　佐内正史写真集

新たなる凝視　中平馬高志・輝　Babylon

定本 木村伊兵衛

森村泰昌展 1996　横浜美術館

土方巽舞踏大鑑（かさぶたとキャラメル）　青幻舎

東京 都市の視線　畠山直哉　伊東豊雄　東京都写真館　LITTLE MORE

金村修写真集　OSIRIS

写真の世紀　THE SIGN OF LIFE　SEINO YOSHIKO　OSAMU KANEMURA　STRATEGY

朝鮮 三十八度線の北　写真・文 久保田博二　東京都写真美術館 1997　教育社

JAPANESE PHOTOGRAPHY TODAY AND ITS PAST　Christopher Phillips　Noriko Fuku

LA COMPARSA

FABIO FABIANO DÍAZ? JOAQUIN GOMEZ BAS

Jacundo de Zurita parana na anga

SELECCIÓN NATURAL | alex dorfsman

GUADALUPE GAONA

Gustavo Carlos Mendía
CHIMENEAS

ESTEBAN PASTORINO

Guido Indij
sin palabras
speechless
ph15
fotografías por chicas de ciudad oculta

FRANCESCA NOCIVELLI
MARAVILHA

Fotógrafos en Buenos Aires
HORACIO CLEMENTE
MÁRIO DE ANDRADE FOTÓGRAFO E TURISTA APRENDIZ
LA AZOHEA
tempo d'imagem

HUMANARIO: Facio · D'Amico · Cortázar

GEOGRAFIA DE PABLO NERUDA
NERUDA
FACIO
DAMICO

¿VIVEREMOS EN LA DEMOCRACIA?

S. MAKARIUS · BUENOS AIRES Y SU GENTE

Buenos Aires · osa ciudad

O
DOMINGOS Ramiro Chaves

SARA FACIO

HORACIO COPPOLA
Galería Jorge Mara · La Ruche
EL BUENOS AIRES DE HORACIO COPPOLA

ARGENTINA en marcha

BUENOS AIRES

35 Dramáticos días

STILL

RM

la marca
editora

argentina

BRAZIL

PIERDOM

IS BRITAIN GREAT? THE CARAVAN GALLERY

SIMON ROBERTS

DEWI LEWIS PUBLISHING

CONSTABLE'S CORNFIELD

QUARITCH

RICHARD BILLINGHAM

RICHARD BILLINGHAM ZOO

BLACK COUNTRY

RICHARD BILLINGHAM

ROGER MAYNE AT 80 A CREEMATORY EXHIBITION OF PHOTOGRAPHS

Ray's a laugh

THEPUBLIC

VIVID

SCALO

DEEDS NOT WORDS

PORT GLASGOW PHOTOGRAPHS BY MARK NEVILLE

Richard Billingham

agnès b.

NIKON GALLERY

Superstructure Mark Power

MARK NEVILLE

HarperCollins Illustrated

photographies de photographs <br> photographs de photographies
 Mark Power

THE TREASURY PROJECT MARK POWER PHOTOWORKS

THE SOUND OF TWO SONGS MARK POWER

The Shipping Forecast

MELODIA DWOCH PIESNI

26 Different Endings Mark Power

Photographs by Mark Power

photoworks

CHRIS KILLIP PIRELLI WORK

Here comes Everybody

steidl

Here Comes Everybody CHRIS KILLIP'S IRISH PHOTOGRAPHS

CHRIS KILLIP'S IRISH PHOTOGRAPHS

photoworks

HEARTS of DARKNESS DON McCULLIN

Donald McCullin

Donald McCullin
 The Destruction Business

Donald McCullin
 The Destruction Business

OPEN SKIES

McCULLIN

McCULLIN

Is Anyone Taking Any Notice?

Is Anyone Taking Any Notice? McCullin

Dimbleby

Don McCullin Perspectives

Don McCullin INDIA

DON McCULLIN

BEIRUT: A CITY IN CRISIS DON McCULLIN

Don McCullin Sleeping with Ghosts

JARRAP

SHAPED BY WAR

DON McCULLIN

DON McCULLIN

MUSEUM

DON McCULLIN IN ENGLAND

DON McCULLIN

Gruvarbetare i Wales Kjell-Åke Andersson / Mikael Wiström

dirty work

Dirty work / light

DAS INDIEN-BUCH PHOTOGRAPHIE IN INDIEN

Tim Heuvelin / Dieter Koeve (Hg.)

Edition Folkwang / Steidl

AKTUEL FOTOGRAFBOK

9

SEACOAL CHRIS KILLIP

Steidl GwinZegal

IN FLAGRANTE CHRIS KILLIP

Isle of Man

Vague à l'âme

Christopher Killip

Marx Mills

Secker & Warburg

IN FLAGRANTE CHRIS KILLIP

Arts Council of Great Britain

Secker & Warburg

Paul Graham

Paul Graham

Paul Graham

Europe: America

England Uncensored

Peter Dench

emphas.is

BEYOND CARING

TROUBLED LAND

PAUL GRAHAM

PAUL GRAHAM

GREY EDITIONS

PAUL GRAHAM

Paul Graham PAINTINGS

End of an Age

SCALO

Ed Ruscha

JO STEFFENS: It appears that you have every book J. G. Ballard wrote. What is your attraction to this writer that the *Atlantic* has called "the catastrophist"?

ED RUSCHA: Ballard is one of the few writers to explore the world of unease, or the unease in the world. He dissects the ills in our life with amazing observations. He is both subtle and obvious at the same time; while introducing an apocalyptic element, he then throws in some tenderness.

You have a collection of books with fore-edge paintings, and you have painted on the covers of books; can you tell us about your interest in the book as a kind of canvas?

I certainly judge books by their covers, but once the dust jacket is off, it enters a strange world of blankness. The flash is in the jacket, and when that's off, what's left over can be seen trembling and exposed and having to rely on its neutered pile of language. The simple act of flipping pages like it's a finger event has always been fulfilling, even if to just smell the pages. I'll never understand how bookbinder

artists of the fourteenth century ever had the idea to paint images on the fore edges of books. They later treated them as secret objects and hid some of the painting within and at the edges of the paper. This is its tradition. My early paintings depicted words, or "titles," and these words were painted again on the sides of the canvas as though it was the spine of a book with the word, say "Damage," being the title of a novel I had authored. To me, this made the book both imaginary and sculptural.

If book collections can tell us something about the mind of their owner, what do you think your library says about you?

The typical thought is of a pipe-smoking robe-and-slippers gentleman drinking wine and smelling the fine leather bindings while his dog sleeps in the corner. Very few of my books are made of leather, and first editions were never in my library. My collection, besides book books, includes leaflets, magazines, single sheets, and oddball printed matter, with most books about artists (about two thousand volumes) from A to Z.

Have you ever had to downsize your book collection? If so, how did you decide which books to discard, what did you do with them, and were there books you wish you had kept?

Today there is a rash of lavish pictorial puff books in the world. There is much repetition in the books on the history of photography in particular. Most of my downsizing begins here.

Can you tell us about the books you selected for your top-ten list, or maybe pick a couple to talk about? If you could add one more book to the list, what would it be?

My selection of top-ten books is not a fixed list. It will always change, if only for novelty's sake. Books are not simply great literature of the world, but sometimes monetarily worthless objects that command my attention. A catalog from a sawmill with pages made of veneer slices of the wood for sale becomes a treasure. A metal-bound book with blank pages is as noteworthy as a volume of Shakespeare. This helps me realize that books are not just carriers of great thought but are also stacks of pages all strapped and connected together. Around 1970 I discovered, quite accidentally, a book entitled *The Changing Mile*. The authors, [James Rodney] Hastings and [Raymond M.] Turner, themselves, had discovered a large collection of glass-plate negatives from the period 1833 to 1962, depicting various desert scenes, together with their exact camera positions. The authors then (sixty years later) rephotographed each scene from the original camera positions and added extensive botanical notations so as to describe the passage of time. This was a monumental discovery for me. To add to this immense curiosity, a recent publication by the same authors, *The Changing Mile, Revisited*, shows the same scenes further studied. This should be a certified work in progress; a monument to the passage of time. This is one of the most important books in my library. *The Log from the Sea of Cortez* comes from our author and national treasure John Steinbeck. Here he sidesteps his usual fictional material to explore, in scientific fashion, the findings from a voyage beginning in Monterey, California, south to the tip of Baja California and up the Sea of Cortez in the year 1941. Enough time has passed that this becomes a valuable study on the evolution of flora and fauna, much like *The Changing Mile*.

Tell us about the physical shelves that hold your books. Are they special in any way — custom-made, off-the-shelf, or built-in?

I have two types of bookshelves. The wooden shelves are nonadjustable but work fine, even as I have to scoot the stacks along as new books enter. This is inevitable as the books seem to breed. Additional shelving was based on the exact product used in the City of Santa Monica Library. These shelves are adjustable, an advantage in many ways.

Is there one book that stands out as having had a huge impact on you when you first read it?

The Americans, by Robert Frank. Around 1958 (also corresponding timewise to the publication of *On the Road* by Jack Kerouac) my friends and I discovered a new book in a store at LA City College. We were all attending Chouinard Art Institute [now CalArts], and a book like *The Americans* had an instant impact. I remember it being a struggle for six young men to view this book at the same time. We all fought over having personal time with this book. It was a revelation and a revolution in a new way to see America. *Dada: Monograph of a Movement* was another discovery by accident. It created an historical portrait of one of the most irreverent art movements of the twentieth century. Art students in general seemed lukewarm to its value as a teaching and historical tool, but I was deeply moved by its contribution to modern art.

Do you agree with the adage "Don't judge a book by its cover?" Or is the design of a book important to you?

In 1992 I was invited by the Getty Museum Library in Santa Monica to visit their vast collection of ancient and modern books, with the idea of selecting and creating an exhibit of volumes of my choice from this extensive trove. Several days were spent reviewing this collection. It was becoming clear that untold numbers of historical books had covers that lacked any kind of embellishment or design applications. Often it was the beauty of parchment or leather or wood that showed in essentially blank covers. Interior subject matter was unimportant or insignificant. My statement for the exhibition brochure is as follows:

> *. . . A BOOK BY ITS COVER*
> *It is considerably worthwhile to study the edges and covers of books which are fundamentally blank. The authors and producers of these books had to resist the temptation to decorate and print images and words on them because covers are so seductive and inviting to artists. Inviting to me personally because I believe each of my own paintings is really a book cover or refers to the possibility of a book cover. A good thing happens when a book is printed with its subject matter concealed. First, it is simpler and in some ways more interesting to have a blank cover for any given book. Secondly, an empty cover has more of a chance of being mysterious and icon-like rather than being an obvious place to advertise its own contents. Finally, there is no such thing as an empty, vacant cover in the sense that stains, ravages of time, accidents, and fingerprints make blank covers never really empty of the visual after all.*

At what age did you begin to seek out books? Did you use the library when you were young?

As odd as it may seem, during high school I had a job with an industrial supply company in Oklahoma City. My task was to visit the central library, and from every phone book in the state I would record each and every lumber company that was in business in Oklahoma. This led to many accidental discoveries of books of all nature.

Top Ten Books
Ed Ruscha

John McPhee,
*Annals of the
Former World*

J. G. Ballard, *Crash*

Chester B. Stem, Inc.,
Eminence in Wood

Jack Kerouac,
On the Road

James Rodney Hast-
ings and Raymond
M. Turner, *The
Changing Mile*

Willy Verkauf, ed.,
*Dada: Monograph of
a Movement*

Miguel de Cervantes,
Don Quixote

John Steinbeck,
*The Log from the
Sea of Cortez*

Sea of Desire
(painted book cover
by Ed Ruscha)

i (painted book cover
by Ed Ruscha)

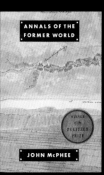

ANNALS OF THE
FORMER WORLD

WINNER OF THE PULITZER PRIZE

JOHN McPHEE

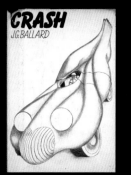

CRASH
J.G. BALLARD

CHESTER B. STEMING.

EMINENCE IN WOOD

STAFF
PICK

JACK KEROUAC
On the Road

the CHANGING
MILE

HASTINGS AND TURNER

DADA

Die Pleite

391

dada

fmsbw tözäu
?mii

THE BLIND MAN

DADA

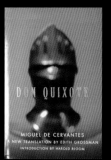

DON QUIXOTE

MIGUEL DE CERVANTES
A NEW TRANSLATION BY EDITH GROSSMAN
INTRODUCTION BY HAROLD BLOOM

JOHN STEINBECK

The Log from
the Sea of Cortez

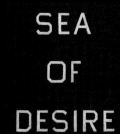

SEA
OF
DESIRE

THE RAB BALLADS — W. S. Gilbert

THE GLASS KEY — DASHIELL HAMMETT

THE RIVER SWIMMER — JIM HARRISON

the Quotable Hitchens — from ALCOHOL to ZIONISM the very best of CHRISTOPHER HITCHENS — WINDSOR MANN

Mortality — Christopher Hitchens

FALLING ANGEL — William Hjortsberg

After Many a Summer Dies the Swan — Aldous Huxley — BRAVE NEW WORLD — ALDOUS HUXLEY — Harcourt Brace Jovanovich

P. D. JAMES — The MURDER ROOM — An Adam Dalgliesh Mystery

They Is Us — TAMA JANOWITZ

THE CRIMINAL

B S JOHNSON — HOUSE MOTHER NORMAL — New Directions

JAMES JOYCE — Tales Told of Shem and Shaun

IRON W

The Letters of Jack Kerouac to Ed White — Glenn Horowitz Bookseller Inc.

BEAT GENERATION — JACK KEROUAC

VISIONS OF CODY — JACK KEROUAC — McGraw-Hill

A STRANGER IN THE WORLD — JOHN LENNON

LOVECRAFT — TALES OF THE CTHULHU MYTHOS — ARKHAM HOUSE

& Literature

CHARLES SAATCHI

W. G. SEBALD — THE RINGS OF SATURN

PETER SELZ — PART-TIME SKETCHES OF A LIFE IN ART

WILL *in the* WORLD — STEPHEN GREENBLATT

DRAWINGS OF BRUNO SCHULZ

LETTERS AND DRAWINGS OF BRUNO SCHULZ *Edited by Jerzy Ficowski*

Radical Innocent: UPTON SINCLAIR — Anthony Arthur — RANDOM HOUSE

HARRY SMITH — THE AVANT-GARDE IN THE AMERICAN VERNACULAR — Perchuk and Singh, Eds.

JUST KIDS | PATTI SMITH

DANGEROUSLY FUNNY — DAVID BIANCULLI

Mr. S — MY LIFE WITH FRANK SINATRA — GEORGE JACOBS AND WILLIAM STADIEM — lt

LETTERS FROM LONDON — MARJORIE SUSMAN

WILFRED THESIGER — Arabian Sands — PENGUIN CLASSICS

It's All About the Dress — Vicky Tiel — ST MARTIN'S PRESS

Jon Krakauer — WHERE MEN WIN GLORY — THE ODYSSEY OF PAT TILLMAN

Titian — THE LAST DAYS — MARK HUDSON — WALKER

Memoirs & Biographies

NORMAN LEAR
Even *This* I Get to Experience

ALAN LOMAX
a biography
JOHN SZWED

ALAN LOMAX
THE MAN WHO...

Barry Lopez
About This Life

BARRY LOPEZ
ARCTIC DREAMS
SCRIBNERS

Conqueror
of the Seas
The Story of Magellan

AMERICAN CHARACTER
THOMPSON
ARCADE

STEVE MARTIN
CRUEL SHOES
PUTNAM

ISAAC NEWTON
JAMES GLEICK

BORN STANDING UP
Steve Martin

AMERICAN PROMETHEUS
THE TRIUMPH AND TRAGEDY OF J. ROBERT
OPPENHEIMER
KAI BIRD
and
MARTIN J. SHERWIN
KNOPF

PAINE
DAVID FREEMAN HAWKE
Harper & Row

DOWN THE GREAT UNKNOWN
John Wesley Powell's 1869 Journey of Discovery and Tragedy Through the Grand Canyon
EDWARD DOLNICK

Nicholas
The Glorious Failure of an American Director
Mysterious Objects: Portraits of Joan Quinn
Patrick McGilligan

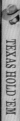

Carrie Mae Weems

JO STEFFENS: Your photographic work incorporates family stories, autobiography, documentary, and other narrative forms. What do you consider to be your role as a storyteller?

CARRIE MAE WEEMS: In the past I've employed elements of text in and around my work, but I'm certainly not a storyteller; storytelling requires skills that I don't possess. Rather, in my work, text functions as a conceptual frame for creating play, counterpoint, tension and/or positioning meaning. The word is a form and the shape of things.

Is there one book that stands out as having had a big impact on you when you first read it?

Books are my playmates, my best friends, my running buddies, my partners in crime, my solace, and my occasional lover. For many years I carried a Felix Gonzalez-Torres catalog [text by Nancy Spector, for the Guggenheim Museum] everywhere; I'd find myself hugging it, holding it tightly to my chest. I fell in love with it—I took simple pleasure in opening it, letting the pages fall where they may, and reading it randomly. I really do love that book; the way it feels, and the way it carries, the ease at which you can move through it, thumb through it, look at it. One day I opened it up and I thought, this is really interesting; who designed this? His name is Takaaki Matsumoto. I was lucky enough to have him design the catalog from my exhibit at the Guggenheim, and we have become wonderful friends. His designs are elegant, smart, and very simple, with beautiful paper.

Do you believe that books can have a special kind of power over us, and if so, what is it about books that have this effect?

Music and books have saved my life. They anchor my being, ground my existence, widen the path, feed and nourish, and the best reveal both the limits and the expanse of our humanity—they are powerful objects. Most books are, however, one-night stands; one rarely goes back for seconds. Of course, then there are those that are returned to again and again, because you can't get enough.

On the subject of rereading, Vladimir Nabokov commented, "We have no physical organ (as we have the eye in regard to a painting) that takes in the whole picture and then can enjoy its details. But at a second, or third, or fourth reading we do, in a sense, behave towards a book as we do towards a painting." Which books do you reread most often, or keep going back to; which writers do you return to?

I've gone back to Ira Glass to reread certain stories. I've gone back to Malcolm Gladwell many times to read the way he enters a story; I am fascinated by the way he leads a reader into the story, the structure of his writing. At first glance you might think they are telling offbeat stories, but they're really not; I think it's really about how the story is constructed, and how they engage with us, they are built in exceptional ways, that's how they set themselves apart. I reread the opening five or six paragraphs of Gladwell's *New Yorker* piece on Edward Snowden and Daniel Ellsberg ["Daniel Ellsberg, Edward Snowden, and the Modern Whistle-Blower," 2016] probably ten times. I thought it was magnificent— what an opening, what a grand way of getting me into this headspace of yours. I've gone back to [J. M.] Coetzee many times because in particular I think *Disgrace* is amazing. I have read Toni Morrison on my knees, just floored by her amazing ability to tap into that thing that is so difficult for most of us. And then Maria Semple—I keep going back to *Where'd You Go, Bernadette*; it's so fantastic, so beautifully constructed out of e-mails. And there are the artists that I return to repeatedly; there's a whole list of them, from the great classical painters to the great modernist painters. Duchamp is one of the great puzzles of my life. I've gone to see Duchamp's work in the Philadelphia Museum more times than I can count. I look into that world he has created for us that is so frightening and exceptionally extraordinary. The wonderful thing about reading is discovering, and going back to, and reinvestigating the people you admire, or have questions about, or that interest or engage you in some way. Or people who have managed to articulate reality for you in a way that you completely get, that you have never been able to say yourself. Tobias Woolf I think is also kind of amazing, and

Cormac McCarthy is really something; his world. There are these passages of language that I find so amazing; and [James] Baldwin, Paul Auster, these authors are really quite special. They have a facility with the language that I so envy and like having close to me.

Are there publishers whose books you covet, or authors or artists you collect? Do you collect certain books because of their beautiful design?

Even though I mark in my books, I prefer beautifully printed books with cotton paper, with strong spines, good color, nice patterns—books that were made with thoughtful consideration, that aren't too big, and can be held easily in the hand. On the other hand I love newsprint; so there is something about rough-and-tumble paper, a kind of throwaway paper that I also really love. I've done projects with newsprint over the years; I love working with it, I love the color of it, that kind of yellow, so I have worked in that way too, but I really do like certain kinds of materials, and those materials

I come back to again and again. And I suppose in some small way this idea of the surface and texture, what a page feels like when you engage with it, is also meaningful because I am a photographer, somebody who is used to working with certain kinds of textures that resonate with the quality of words and pictures in a certain kind of way. So this material, and the material world, is one I think we all are deeply engaged in. And how we are engaged in that, how I am engaged in that, really matters to me. What's around me, what do I build, what do I look at, what do I touch, what do I enjoy touching— that tactile nature of reading and looking at books is as important as reading them. Most of us have books that we will never read. It's all sort of wishful thinking—I keep looking at my books and think, when am I going to read that, when is it possible?

If you could design or customize your library, and there were no restrictions, is there anything you would change?

If I could, I'd have a very large room filled with books on the floors, wall to wall and floor to ceiling. In the center would be a chair just for me, along with a small table for pads, pencils, and ashtrays. This would be my playroom, and every day from 4:00 to 7:00 p.m., I'd have tea, or martinis, with my closest friends.

Regarding your recent performance-based work, you have stated, "There are only a few great stories in the world and they are repeated again and again." How did you come to create this work?

For many years, even though I have not done any theater, I was always interested in theater to one degree or another. So I decided about a year ago that I would spend some time reading about Brecht again. (I go back to Beckett, to *Waiting for Godot,* over and over and over; it's the thing I constantly reread, I read it several times a year.) So I was looking at Bertolt Brecht because I wanted to understand it, and I was thinking about theater while mounting *Grace Notes* [*Grace Notes: Reflections for Now,* a performance of music, song, text, spoken word, and video projection, premiered at the Spoleto Festival in June 2016]. It was really through reading some early work about Brecht that I realized that I myself was actually building the story of Antigone; that I was creating a modern-day Antigone as Brecht did in his day. I didn't realize I was working on Antigone until I was reading about Brecht's work. It was through this that I discovered my own self, and I think that's what reading is. I was just so stunned when I realized I had created a contemporary Antigone. This idea that there are only a couple of stories and they get retold again and again and again, I think is true. There are these themes, and Antigone has a great theme; a sister wants to bury her brother with honor, that's all she wants to do. But in a larger community that denies her that right, and in a state that denies her that right. So if we look at that contemporarily, we can extrapolate pretty easily, it's not difficult. There's that wonderful song by Billie Holiday, "The Same Old Story," [sings], "It's all fun and laughter, They lived ever after in ecstasy, The same old story but it's new to me." I was deeply affected when I learned that

indeed I had actually tapped into an old story, an ancient story.

Do you read for pleasure, out of curiosity, or professionally? Are there certain books that have helped you in your own work?

Reading is a way of searching for meaning, a way to self-discovery, a point of departure for figuring things out, or for mapping a process. I think I do it because I am searching; it is not just for pleasure, but it is the searching out and the seeking of greater understanding of myself through what others have made. For me, reading is always related to work, to effort, to discovery. It has something to do with understanding that somebody else has been there; somebody else has charted a path. It's not the path that you're going to take—you have to take your own—but your path can certainly be informed by what has been made, what has come before you, and who has struggled through it. While I take great pleasure in reading, I don't read for pleasure. I'm too hungry, too desperate; like everybody else

I'm stumbling through the darkness, looking for the light—and for a flash, a hot minute, certain writers/books illuminate the darkness, for which I am eternally grateful.

**Top Ten Books
Carrie Mae Weems**

Henri Cartier-
Bresson, *The
Decisive Moment*

Marcel Griaule,
*Conversations
with Ogotemmêli:
An Introduction to
Dogon Religious
Ideas*

Sander L. Gilman,
*Difference and
Pathology: Stereo-
types of Sexuality,
Race, and Madness*

Nancy Spector, *Felix
Gonzalez-Torres*

Zora Neale Hurston,
*Their Eyes Were
Watching God*

Mario Varas Llosa,
*In Praise of the
Stepmother*

Ronald T. Takaki,
*Iron Cages: Race
and Culture in 19th-
Century America*

J. M. Coetzee, *Inner
Workings: Literary
Essays, 2000–2005*

James Baldwin,
*The Evidence of
Things Not Seen*

Deborah Willis,
*Reflections in Black:
A History of Black
Photographers, 1840
to the Present*

Roy DeCarava and
Langston Hughes,
*The Sweet Flypaper
of Life*

Conversations
with
Ogotemmêli

AN INTRODUCTION TO DOGON
RELIGIOUS IDEAS

MARCEL GRIAULE

SANDER L. GILMAN

ZORA NEALE
HURSTON

Their Eyes Were
Watching God

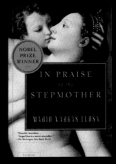

NOBEL PRIZE
WINNER

IN PRAISE
of the
STEPMOTHER

MARIO VARGAS LLOSA

"Powerful, incendiary...
Vargas Llosa is a master storyteller."
—*The Washington Post Book World*

Iron Cages

Race and Culture in 19th-Century America

Ronald T. Takaki

WINNER OF THE NOBEL PRIZE

J. M. Coetzee

INNER WORKINGS

LITERARY ESSAYS

ZADIE SMITH

SAUL BELLOW
W. G. SEBALD
PAUL CELAN
HUGO CLAUS
GABRIEL GARCÍA MÁRQUEZ NADINE
GORDIMER · GÜNTER GRASS · GRAHAM
GREENE · SÁNDOR MÁRAI
ROBERT MUSIL · V. S. NAIPAUL
PHILIP ROTH · BRUNO
SCHULZ · ITALO SVEVO
ROBERT WALSER · WALT WHITMAN

JAMES
BALDWIN
THE
EVIDENCE
OF THINGS
NOT SEEN

WITH A NEW INTRODUCTION
AND PREFACE BY THE AUTHOR

REFLECTIONS IN
BLACK

DEBORAH WILLIS

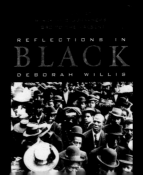

THE SWEET
FLYPAPER
OF LIFE

Roy DeCarava and Langston Hughes

hen the bicycle of the Lord bearing
His messenger with a telegram for
Sister Mary Bradley saying "Come home" arrived at 113
West 134th Street, New York City, Sister Bradley said, "Boy,
take that wire right on back to St. Peter because I am not
prepared to go. I might be a little sick, but as yet I ain't
no ways tired." And she would not even sign for the message
—since she had tried it first, while claiming she could not find
(continued on page 3)

STILES AND SELZ

A SOURCEBOOK OF ARTISTS' WRITINGS

THEORIES AND DOCUMENTS OF CONTEMPORARY ART

California

MICHELLE OBAMA

MICHAEL ONDAATJE — Anil's Ghost

FAZAL SHEIKH — RAMADAN MOON

GABRIEL GARCIA MARQUEZ — Strange Pilgrims

Observations on the Colony of LOUISIANA from 1796 to 1802 — PITOT

SLAVES IN THE FAMILY — EDWARD BALL

The New Negro — Edited by Alain Locke — Atheneum

TA-NEHISI COATES | BETWEEN THE WORLD AND ME

english : each : hour : redeem — time and justice in african american literature

english : each : hour : redeem — time and justice in african american literature

THE VENUS HOTTENTOT — ELIZABETH ALEXANDER

SUZUKI — Zen Mind, Beginner's Mind

FILM CULTURE — No. 65–66 — 1978

Meyer Schapiro — Mondrian: On the Humanity of Abstract Painting

Wounded in the House of a Friend — Sonia Sanchez — George Braziller

FREUD — Civilization and its Discontents — NORTON

KARL MARX — THE CIVIL WAR IN FRANCE

HOLD IT AGAINST ME — DOYLE

CONSTRUCTING MASCULINITY — Berger / Wallis / Watson — ROUTLEDGE

LANTERNS — MARIAN WRIGHT EDELMAN

Tomkins — Living Well Is the Best Revenge

Sahakian — IDEAS OF THE GREAT PHILOSOPHERS — BARNES & NOBLE

SEEING POWER — NATO THOMPSON

ART IN THE PUBLIC INTEREST — RAVEN

CULTURALLY RESPONSIVE TEACHING — THEORY, RESEARCH, AND APPLICATION — SECOND EDITION

GAY

THE ONE and THE MANY — GRANT H. KESTER

Dialogues in Public Art — Finkelpearl

THE BLACK PHOTOGRAPHERS ANNUAL   VOLUME 4   ANOTHER VIEW, INC.

DeCARAVA/HUGHES   THE SWEET FLYPAPER OF LIFE

DIANE ARBUS   Patricia Bosworth

WOMEN AND ART   JUDY CHICAGO AND
CONTESTED TERRITORY   EDWARD LUCIE-SMITH

CLAUDIA RANKINE   CITIZEN   Graywolf Press

THE FIRST BAD MAN   A NOVEL BY MIRANDA JULY

THE REPEATING BODY   KIMBERLY JUANITA BROWN   DUKE

Nooter

BARBARA CHASE-RIBOUD   EVERY TIME A KNOT IS UN-DONE A GOD IS RE-LEAS-ED   COLLECTED AND NEW POEMS 1974-2011

Roy DeCarava   A Retrospective

A CENTURY OF AFRICAN AMERICAN ART   AMAKI

City Art   New York's Percent for Art Program

FINEBERG   ART SINCE 1940   STRATEGIES OF BEING   Second Edition

POWELL ET AL.   RHAPSODIES IN BLACK   ART OF THE HARLEM RENAISSANCE   CALIFORNIA   IniVA   Hayward Gallery

GRAY   MICHAEL JACKSON   BEFORE HE WAS

Theaster Gates   My Labor Is My Protest

12 BALLADS FOR HUGUENOT HOUSE   THEASTER GATES

ROBERT FRANK   THE AMERICANS   APERTURE

PABLO PICASSO: A RETROSPECTIVE   THE MUSEUM OF MODERN ART   NEW YORK

secrecy   african art that conceals and reveals   The Museum for African Art   Prestel

GERHARD RICHTER OCTOBER 18, 1977   STORR   The Museum of Modern Art

Show and Tell   A Chronicle of Group Material   Edited by Julie Ault   Four Corners Books

DAWOUD BEY   Picturing People   THE RENAISSANCE SOCIETY

Witkovsky   Dawoud Bey: Harlem, U.S.A.   Yale

BORIS FRIEDEWALD   WOMEN PHOTOGRAPHERS   PRESTEL

Lepik   Small Scale, Big Change: New Architectures of Social Engagement   MoMA

SOTHEBY'S   New York   Sale 6003   Photographs from the Collection of Graham Nash   April 25, 1990

YASUMASA MORIMURA   DAUGHTER OF ART HISTORY   APERTURE

ETCHED IN COLLECTIVE HISTORY   BIRMINGHAM MUSEUM OF ART

HAYNES   The Bearden Project   THE STUDIO MUSEUM IN HARLEM

Sills   IN REAL LIFE: SIX WOMEN PHOTOGRAPHERS   Holiday House

INSIDE THE VISIBLE   an elliptical traverse of 20th century art   in, of, and from the feminine   de Zegher, editor

BGC YALE   Knoll Textiles   Nineteenhundredfortyfive – Twothousandten

THE MUSEUM OF MODERN ART NEW YORK

MERRELL

ABRAMS

sbc

Daedalus
stone canoe
stone canoe
Urban Folklore from the Paperwork Empire
POSITIVELY BLACK
BARBARA CHASE-RIBOUD
EVERY-TIME A KNOT IS UN-DONE, A GOD IS RE-LEAS-ED
Hottentot Venus
BARBARA CHASE-RIBOUD
RESIDENT'S DAUGHTER
ASPHALT
CARL HANCOCK RUX
KURT VONNEGUT
Paolo Giordano
The Solitude of Prime Numbers
bell hooks
WOUNDS OF PASSION
LISA DELPIT
THE SKIN THAT WE SPEAK
J. M. Coetzee
INNER WORKINGS
LITERARY ESSAYS
J M COETZEE
Life & Times of Michael K
J. M. Coetzee
Diary of a Bad Year
ART OF GRACE
On Moving Well Through Life
SARAH L. KAUFMAN
Their Eyes Were Watching God
Zora Neale Hurston
THE FLAMETHROWERS
RACHEL KUSHNER

Contributors

Janet Cardiff and George Bures Miller are internationally renowned installation and sound artists. Their breakthrough work was 1995's *The Dark Pool*, a roomful of bric-a-brac that made noises as viewers passed by and interacted with it. This set the tone for subsequent work, which had viewers confronting the uncanny by way of ambiguous objects and fractured narratives. Cardiff and Miller represented Canada at the Venice Biennale in 2001, with *The Paradise Institute* receiving a special jury prize, the first to be presented to Canadians at the Biennale.

Painter, writer, and musician Billy Childish, born William Hamper in 1959, in Chatham, England, has recorded over 150 LPs and published over 45 volumes of poetry and 5 novels; his paintings are now exhibited by major galleries and collected around the world. He was included in *British Art Show 5*, which toured throughout the UK, and has been the subject of major survey exhibitions at the ICA in London and White Columns in New York, and more recently in 2015 at the Opelvillen Foundation, Germany. He continues to live and work in Rochester/Chatham, Kent.

Since the mid-1980s, Mark Dion has created sculptures and installations that serve as critiques of institutional power structures, questioning notions of the representation of nature, display, codification, and collecting. For decades, his practice has addressed issues and strategies that are central to much art being produced today. Born in Massachusetts in 1961, Dion currently lives in New York City. He received a BFA and an honorary doctorate from the University of Hartford School of Art, Connecticut, in 1986 and 2003, respectively.

Tracey Emin was born in London in 1963, and studied at Maidstone College of Art and the Royal College of Art, London. She has exhibited extensively internationally, including in solo and group exhibitions in Holland, Germany, Japan, Australia, and America. In 2007 Emin represented Britain at the 52nd Venice Biennale, becoming the second female artist to ever do so. That same year, Emin was made a Royal Academician and was awarded an honorary doctorate from the Royal College of Art, a doctor of letters from the University of Kent, and a doctor of philosophy from London Metropolitan University. In 2011 she became the Royal Academy's Professor of Drawing, and in 2012 Queen Elizabeth II appointed her Commander of the Most Excellent Order of the British Empire for her contributions to the visual arts.

Wangechi Mutu studied at the Cooper Union and Yale University, and has made art in New York for almost twenty years. She is the recipient of the United States Artist Grant (2014) and the Brooklyn Museum's Asher B. Durand Artist of the Year Award (2013), and was honored as Deutsche Guggenheim's first Artist of the Year (2010). Ms. Mutu recently participated in the Venice Biennale: All the World's Futures (2015), and the Dak'Art Biennial (2014). She has exhibited at numerous one-person shows worldwide, including the Deutsche Guggenheim Museum in Berlin, Musée d'Art Contemporain de Montréal, Staatliche Kunsthalle in Baden Baden, the Museum of Contemporary Art in Sydney, the Brooklyn Museum, and the Nasher Museum of Art in Durham, North Carolina, and her work is in the collections of major institutions.

Matthias Neumann is principal at normaldesign and an independent curator.

Martin Parr is one of the best-known documentary photographers of his generation. With over ninety books of his own published, and another thirty he has edited, his photographic legacy is well established. Parr also acts as a curator and editor. He has curated two photography festivals, Arles in 2004 and Brighton Biennial in 2010. In 2016 Parr curated the Barbican exhibition *Strange and Familiar*. Parr has been a member of the Magnum agency since 1994 and is currently the agency's president. His work has been collected by many of the major museums, including the Tate, Pompidou, and the Museum of Modern Art in New York.

Ed Ruscha was born in 1937 in Omaha, Nebraska. He graduated from the Chouinard Art Institute (now CalArts), Los Angeles, in 1960. In a career spanning more than five decades, Ruscha has distilled the archetypal signs and symbols of the American vernacular into typographic and cinematic codes that are as accessible as they are profound. In 2016 the Fine Arts Museums of San Francisco opened *Ed Ruscha and the Great American West*, a major solo exhibition, at the de Young Museum, exploring his attachments to the sights and scenes of the iconic landscape with more than eighty works spanning the artist's career. Ruscha currently lives and works in Los Angeles.

Damion Searls has translated twenty-five books from German, French, Norwegian, and Dutch, by writers including Marcel Proust (*On Reading*), Friedrich Nietzsche (*Anti-Education*), Rainer Maria Rilke (*The Inner Sky: Poems, Notes, Dreams*), and five Nobel Prize winners.

Jo Steffens is a writer, editor, curator, and publisher, former director of the Municipal Art Society of New York's Urban Center Books and Banff-Calgary International Writers Festival, and recipient of the Rozsa Award for Innovation in Arts Management.

Considered one of the most influential contemporary American artists, **Carrie Mae Weems** has investigated family relationships, cultural identity, sexism, class, political systems, and the consequences of power. Weems has sustained an ongoing dialogue within contemporary discourse for over thirty years, developing a complex body of art employing photographs, text, fabric, audio, digital images, installation, and video. She has participated in numerous solo and group exhibitions at major national and international museums, including the Metropolitan Museum of Art, the Frist Center for Visual Art, the Solomon Guggenheim Museum in New York, and the Centro Andaluz de Arte Contemporáneo in Seville, Spain.